THE

MARTYR LAMB

OR

CHRIST

THE REPRESENTATIVE OF HIS PEOPLE IN ALL AGES

TRANSLATED FROM THE GERMAN OF
F. W. KRUMMACHER, D.D.

BAKER BOOK HOUSE
Grand Rapids, Michigan

Reprinted 1978 by
Baker Book House
from the edition issued in 1841
by Robert Carter

ISBN: 0-8010-5394-3

PHOTOLITHOPRINTED BY CUSHING - MALLOY, INC.
ANN ARBOR, MICHIGAN, UNITED STATES OF AMERICA
1978

CONTENTS

THE AUTHOR'S PREFACE

THERE is no superfluity of Biblical Discourses, at least of those in which the great doctrine of Christ being our representative, stands pre-eminent, casting a light upon all others. It was this consideration which overcame the hesitation I felt in publishing the following contemplations. It is with earnest seriousness I send them forth to the world, and I entreat my readers to study them with attention before pronouncing on their merits; and not to cry at random, "Enthusiasm! Hyper-orthodoxy!" I believe that I have drawn from the well of Scripture all that I have taught; and out of Scripture, let those who think I have erred correct me, for I am willing to learn.

It has been said, "As there is nothing so absurd but what some philosopher has taught; so there is nothing presented to a philosopher's attention which he should refuse to try and examine, ere he takes upon him to reject it. Disgust without reason, is a proof either of a diseased appetite, or of an over-indulged and fantastic imagination." The same voice from the desert says, "Hyper-critics are always inquiring what truth is, but at the same moment have their hands on the door; for they will not wait to receive an answer to their question." Again, "Our reason resembless the blind Theban soothsayer, to whom his daughter Manto described the flight of birds; and he prophesied according to her description." In another place, "Since great part of Scripture was written under the direction of God by the humble, the low, and the uneducated, putting to shame the talent and ingenuity of profane writers; so it requires men enlightened by the Spirit of God, whose eyes are jealous as those of a friend, to discern the rays of heavenly glory in such a guise!" These remarks are for the consideration of critics: meanwhile I may assure those who are earnestly seeking after salvation, that many branches of the tree of life are interspersed through this book, from which the Author, during his labours, plucked sweet fruits ripened under other suns. Oh! that the same harvest might be reaped by each of his readers! then the only wish with which he sends forth this book would be granted, and to God on high should be ascribed the glory!

F. W. KRUMMACHER,

Pastor in Gemarke

CHRIST AND THE FIRST SINNERS

"HOSANNA!" Thus let us rejoice to-day, with the multitude who at Christ's entrance into Jerusalem went forth to meet him, with branches of palm in their hands, and strewed their garments in the way! Let us transport ourselves into the midst of the joyful crowd, and witness the scene of our Lord's advent. The cry is already heard, "Who is he that cometh?" And the words, "Help us! Take pity upon us!" resound on every side. Jesus comes, the sinner's Friend—the promised One whom many prophets and kings desired to see, but had not seen. In the name of the Lord, in the place of God, he offers peace and joy to a lost world. He comes as Israel's King to destroy the kingdom of darkness, and to raise a throne of grace upon its ruins. Never did one come like unto him. What are all the triumphal entrances of the great and powerful of this world, when compared to his! Verily, had the people been silent, the stones would have opened their mouths, and the very tiles upon the house-tops would have called out "Hosanna!"

Hosanna! resounds among the people. Why is it

that they shout and rejoice in this manner now? Because he never came before in such pomp and glory. He comes from the grave of Lazarus, as he who has the keys of hell and of death. He comes as described in an ancient prophesy, which is at this moment remembered by the people: "Rejoice greatly, O daughter of Zion; shout, O daughter of Jerusalem; behold, thy King cometh unto thee; he is just, and having salvation; lowly, and riding upon an ass, and upon a colt the foal of an ass!" Glorious anticipations stir within the soul of the multitude, and it is these anticipations make them cry out "Hosanna! Hosanna!"

The voices of his friends are heard, for they rejoice to behold their King in such beauty and glory. The voices of his enemies are heard, though they have a sad presentiment that He is the person who shall one day trample them in the dust. Thus the various voices resound together in one mighty chorus, "Hosanna! blessed is he that cometh in the name of the Lord! Hosanna in the highest!"

Hosanna! had often been cried already. Through every age, from the beginning of the world, we hear the sound of the advent-bell greeting the coming Christ. Let us now employ the present season of Advent profitably, and lend an attentive ear to those beautiful tones throughout the various periods of God's government. Our plan is this. We shall consider Christ as the desire and refuge of sinners—in the infancy of our race—in the still and quiet patriarchal times—in the age of Moses and the giving of the law—during the time of kings and prophets—and lastly, in those latter days which kings and prophets desired to see but only saw afar off. May the blessing of God accompany our meditations!

Genesis iv. 1

"*And Eve bare Cain, and said, I have gotten a man from the Lord.*"

Our journey to-day leads us back to the far-distant, dim, and misty past. The words of the text carry us to the commencing point of the history of our race—to the very threshold of the scarcely closed Paradise. In spirit we pay a visit to our great ancestors; not to be a witness of their misery, but for another and more joyful reason. Though their first glory has passed away, yet a new one shines forth to-day, and casts a halo over their existence. Hark! the advent-bells are chiming over the lost earth! "Christ and the first sinners" is the title of this day's contemplation. To this Christ let us now direct our eyes, and consider him—in the hope of our first parents—in their supposed possession of him—and in their longing and desiring love.

Where is it that we meet our first parents? Alas! we need no longer knock at the gate of the garden of Eden. No longer does the voice of man sound from within; but instead we hear the words thundered forth, "Away from hence!" and the flaming sword of the cherubim presents to us a fearful barrier. The Fall, which draws along with it such disastrous consequences, has taken place; the light of the divine image has been turned into darkness; the decree of Eternal Justice has interposed, and the "murderer from the beginning" is now rejoicing at his own manifold and gigantic triumph. The whole human race have fallen into his snare, and a world lies exposed to his machinations on the lost field of combat. The first created of our race dwell no more in the holy place of God: driven from their Father's house, we meet them to-day upon a soil, over which the Almighty has pronounced the curse of his fierce anger. They rest no longer like beloved and confiding children on the bosom of their Creator; for, alas! sin has been committed; and heaven is now gathering its black clouds over their heads. They who a short time before were the lords of earth and of all that therein is, are now exposed to the fury of the elements; and all the powers of nature seem leagued against them. They who had personal intercourse with Jehovah, who were nourished by his hands, and who received from his table those fruits of life which no earthly tree can now bear,—they must by the sweat of their brow compel the fields to afford them the bread of sorrow; cultivate the stubborn earth, which is more inclined to produce thorns and thistles than the wholesome grain; and, weighed down by cares and sufferings, they must struggle and toil to procure every temporal gratification. Everywhere the sword of the cherub is to be seen. Everywhere they must use force to protect their own lives; and they cannot even defend themselves from the beasts of the field but by destroying or subjecting them. Alas! a curse is upon all, and the universal misery may well give occasion to the wise man's complaint, "For what hath a man of all his labour, and of the vexation of his heart, wherein he hath laboured under the sun? For all his days are sorrows, and his travail grief."

A miserable hut or wanderer's tent hastily put together, is the dwelling in which we now find the former inhabitants of Paradise. They have been obliged to take refuge here; for all nature, as we said before, wields against them a cherub's sword, and persecutes them with cold and storms, hail and thunderbolts. They are clad with the skins of wild animals, and, like ourselves at present, are surrounded by unceasing cares and toils; while death and the grave are hovering in the distance. They might perhaps accommodate themselves to these miserable circumstances, were it not for the terrible contrast between their present and former condition. They are not like those who merely fall from affluence into poverty. Alas! they are kings deprived of their crown, princes and rulers who have exchanged a throne of glory for a bed of straw, a sceptre for a beggar's staff. This remembrance of the bright and beautiful past, must be to them now the bitterest drop in their cup of suffering. The sunshiny splendour, not yet faded away, of the days that are gone, can only serve to show more strikingly the mournful present in all its gloom and darkness. Yet this hard fate might be borne—this host of eternal evils and afflictions might be supported—were it not for the worm within!—the weight upon their conscience—the fearful conviction of having involved their whole posterity along with themselves in destruction—the total change and disorganization of their characters once so perfect—the law of sin in their members—and the feeling in their miserable souls of the divine anger, and of that curse which burns down even into hell! O my God! what overwhelming misery and woe!

How shall we find those unfortunates? Can we find them otherwise than weeping and wringing their hands? Grief must already have almost consumed them, and plunged them in the very abyss of despair. Certainly one might well have expected this. But lo! what do we behold? We step nearer, and find every thing completely different; and the mournful picture which we a moment ago beheld in spirit, has now vanished into air. It is true that Adam, once the king of earth, now labours in the fields, tilling the ground and planting seed, the sweat meanwhile dropping from his brow; nevertheless he is joyful and of good courage, as if he had never known a higher and better condition. Eve, formerly so beautiful and glorious, is now no longer a queen, but, surrounded by cares and toils, she labours within the compass of her narrow dwelling; yet it seems as though she no longer missed the delights of Paradise, for she is as serene and contented as if she had always been accustomed to her present miserable habitation. How different from all we had expected! We should have thought that even in the brilliancy of the morning red, the flaming sword of the cherub would have appeared to them. But no! they salute the coming morn with outstretched arms, and praise the name of the Lord. We should have thought that every morsel of the bread which they eat would be bathed in tears before it reached their mouths. Not so. They eat their bread in silent cheerfulness, and, with smiles of thankfulness on their countenances, look up from the gifts they enjoy, towards their heavenly Giver. It does indeed astonish us to behold in those fallen ones such unexpected composure and serenity. It does not proceed merely from a sense of security, and far less from presumption and defiance of their Creator; but happiness is depicted in every look and every motion, because the divine compassion has been shown, and their God has once more received them. Yes, already the cross shines, though but with a feeble glimmer, through the midst of the clouds which have darkened their early existence. Already, through the night of misery and woe, we can distinguish the joyful words, "There is a rest at hand." In the horizon of the future we see a new Paradise blooming for them; and it seems as though we beheld an angel with a palm branch in his hand passing through their dwellings: for the joyful promise is heard, "A Saviour is coming." Happy for us, we all know this great and glorious word, which in a moment removed the unutterable sorrow of our first parents, and with a hand of power dried up their tears. We know that blessed gospel, which clad their heaven in the brilliant hues of morning, and sounded day and night in their ears, as a clear and joyful advent-bell. Immediately after the Fall, the Almighty consoled the trembling sinners; and opening his mouth, said to the serpent, "I will put enmity between thee and the woman, and between thy seed and her seed; it shall bruise thy head, and thou shalt bruise his heel." Adam and Eve had marked these words; they prized them now as the star of their dreary existence, or as a refreshing brook out of which they might drink deep draughts of consolation and peace, while it flowed through the fields groaning under the curse of their Creator. This promised salvation raised them upon angels' wings far above the annoyances and hardships of their earthly pilgrimage, and enabled them once more thankfully and joyfully to open their hearts to the God from whom they had so mournfully estranged themselves.

"Bless the Lord, O my soul, and forget not all his benefits!" Though I have fallen along with Adam from the height on which I stood, yet have I not received a great salvation! O who would not be willing to live even on this sorrowful earth, when such a God of love has stretched out his arms to save us! It is good for us to reside in this vale of tears, and to encounter the stormy billows of the waters of affliction, since such a Saviour meets us. Though it is dark and gloomy around us, yet the cross of salvation is shining through the clouds. An eternal refuge is opened; the Saviour of sinners has come; and there stands engraved on the pillars of the world a mighty name, "Immanuel." We have but to read this name, when we fall down rejoicing, and no longer regret the lost Paradise.

II. Let us principally contemplate Eve, who now approaches us with such a mysterious and joyful air,

that we cannot for a moment doubt that something altogether unprecedented either has happened to her, or is about to happen. The radiancy which illumines her countenance, and betokens so much internal happiness, was never hitherto observed on her features. The commotion of thought and feeling, in which we find her to-day, is not the customary voice of her heart. What is it, then, that elevates her so, and renders her so joyful and glad? Is it the anticipation of the mother's happiness, which is to be hers so shortly? Yes, my brethren, it is so, but in a very different sense from what you may imagine. Her delight is far above that of women, for her expectation has a more glorious object. She and her husband both imagine they behold a star of hope beaming in their humble dwelling. Eve's anticipations are the same as Mary's were long ages after. She hopes that, although she has involved her whole posterity along with herself in destruction, yet that she is the person who shall present to them the Restorer and Saviour of the world; and that, instead of cursing her, the children of men shall revere her as the mother of Him through whom they shall all be made alive.

Eve's hour is come; and that is fulfilled which the Lord had spoken, "In sorrow thou shalt bring forth children." Cain comes into the world in the midst of pain and suffering—but his mother disregards all this, for her soul is filled with blissful anticipations. As the babe rests upon its mother's lap, what stupendous thoughts pass through her mind! Her countenance is illumined like that of a glorified saint. She regards the little being before her with an emotion such as only one mother since that time has hailed her infant. It is not motherly joy alone; it is veneration, devotion, and heavenly rapture, with which she greets her first-born—her soul meanwhile crying, Hosanna! Can she do otherwise, when she believes that the child whom she holds in her arms is God? Yes—God! She thinks that she has borne the "seed of the woman" which is to bruise the serpent's head; for how should she know the times of the Lord? She believes that it is the Messiah, the Lord of glory, who now rests upon her breast; that the promised Mediator and Saviour is now her son, a new and better shoot from the decaying tree. He is to be her justification: the mother does not carry the child, but the child carries the mother upward along with himself into the third heaven. Is this child Immanuel? She believes it firmly; and, enraptured with this idea, she calls out, "I have gotten a man from the Lord," or, as it may be rendered, "I have the man Jehovah!" Does she err in this? Alas! my brethren, she does err. The scene is most moving and heart-touching. Of what avail is it that we call out, "Eve! awake from this sweet dream!" or what good does it do that we say to her, "Alas! dost thou not see that no glory shines round the head of the child, no angels sing over his cradle, no salutation from on high comes to greet his advent?" She will not awaken from this blissful, though wonderful delusion. She remains fixed in her idea, and shouts for joy, "I have gotten the man, the Lord—the man Jehovah!" But again I say, how can she imagine that she has the Almighty God as a naked child on her lap, and that the Lord of glory reclines on her breast? We are almost ready to reject the idea as strange and unnatural; until we remember that in truth and reality a mortal mother did once look upon her infant and say, "I have gotten the man Jehovah!" and that Eve's bold dream four thousand years later was realized. Know ye not Bethlehem—the Virgin, that blessed among women—the message of the angel Gabriel—and the Babe in the manger? Over his cradle all the morning stars shouted for joy; in his hands rested the sceptre of the world and the palm-branch of grace and peace.

Are we not happy that we have seen this miracle of compassion and eternal love? It is for us to say, "I have the man Jehovah!" And what fulness of riches, what plenitude of blessings does not this sentence express! If we have this possession, what more can we desire? We have, then, God's righteousness for a garment, God's love for a resting-place, God's power to make us conquer, God's shield for a covering, God's gracious eye for a sun, and God's heaven for an inheritance. Yes, this is a possession for which the angels might well envy us. *I have*—it is not *I have had*—nor yet is it *I shall have*—no, it is *I have!* When I can say this, then all which I possess henceforward is but dust and ashes; I need nothing more, for the eternal heights are my inheritance. No one can mistake the child reposing on the lap of the king's daughter: *He is the man Jehovah.* He himself will demonstrate it to you all. He will write it in your lives in ineffacable characters—to some He will do it with his right hand, plucking them as brands from the burning, and raising them up into heaven—to others with his left hand, condemning them, and casting them into eternal fire, the dwelling-place of the devil and his angels.

III. Eve, the mother of all living, believed that the helpless little infant on her lap was the Man Jehovah. What bright views did not this idea give of the mysterious dignity of man, of the eternal counsel of reconciliation, and of the mediatorship of the promised Pledge! The first sinners required to look thus deeply into the secrets of God, to save themselves from the consciousness of their own gigantic guilt, and to keep from sinking in despair, under the weight of the misery they had brought upon themselves. We cannot, therefore, blame the poor mother for grasping so boldly the mighty consolation. It was not too early for the light of the new testament to shine upon her. God knows neither times nor seasons in the fulfilment of his promises, but gives to his chosen ones acording as they have need. They who had walked with God and had fellowship with him, as one friend with another, were also much more capable of comprehending the incarnation of a God than their descendants. But alas! the babe in Eve's arms was not the Man Jehovah, as she supposed: we can see the angels looking mournfully on his cradle —for it is the murderer Cain, and this the poor mother quickly learns.

Although she grieves deeply when she discovers her error, yet her grief is but a small price for the moments of rapture she experienced while her sweet dream lasted. Although she had been mistaken with regard to her boy, and although he was not to prove the promised "seed of the woman," yet when she discovered her error, the Man Jehovah was not taken away from her; it was only changing the supposed object of present possession into the object of hope and expectation for the future. She would now know from her own experience, what it is to have attained the promised goal. Oh! had she not been happy in her child! With what heavenly rapture had she cradled the boy in her arms, and pressed him to her bosom; her conscience for the moment becoming pure and light as that of the infant on her lap! The consciousness of sin ceased to weigh down her soul, for her heart rejoiced in the realization of God's unutterable mercy. She felt that, justified and righteous, she could now rest on the bosom of her God; that she had a possession which amply repaid her for the loss of Paradise; and that she had been transported into a new and more beautiful Eden. Yet she has no reason to regret those sweet thoughts and experiences, though her imagination clothed them far too soon with reality. The Divine promise sounds now more beautiful than ever in her delighted ears; for higher than formerly she knows how to prize that immeasurable grace which in deed and in truth had promised to send the object of our hope—God become man. Free from all grovelling earthly thoughts as heretofore, her hopes and desires are still directed towards her little treasure, which now seems a type of the heavenly one; and more ardently than ever she calls out from the bottom of her soul, "O thou that comest down from heaven, descend speedily!"

If we regard the spiritual life of Eve, we see that in faith and love she moved out of Advent into the sweet light of Christmas; and that out of Christmas she retraced her steps into Advent again, although into a far more blessed one than the first. If God but once manifest himself unto us—if he enable us in our hearts to feel and know him as he is, "the man Jehovah,"—then the joyful and the true Advent begins. Formerly we stood trembling and afflicted, we sought help and found none. We looked behind us—alas! there lay paradise, now for ever closed, the inexorable cherub guarding its gates. We examined our own bosoms—woe unto us! sin, and the curse of God, were raging there, and we found nothing but weakness and frailty. We looked upon the mountains—dark clouds enveloped their summits, amidst which awful thunders were rolling; and we could only cry out, "O God, thine eye seeth us, therefore we die." We beheld all around arrayed against us—nothing could be seen but the sword of the cherub—nothing but wrath and destruction. We directed our gaze towards the distance—there, shadowy forms were threatening us—death, judgment, and the fiery terrors of hell. Whatever refuge we sought, we only found despair. Lo! who is it comes to meet us, surrounded as we are by the terrors of night? Who is it that accosts us with the salutation of love? Who is it that calls to us, "Be consoled, for I come!" It is the good Shepherd, the Prince of Peace, the Ruler of the storm; and our hour of salvation has arrived. No sooner does the sinner's Friend enlighten our poor hearts with his glances of love—no sooner does he permit us to rest on his bosom —than our whole existence is changed; our dwelling-place is no longer here below; we cannot endure to remain at a distance from him; our hearts seem attracted by a heavenly magnet, for they burn to escape, and to rush, though it may be over rocks and mountains, towards him. The springs of our life flow to him as surely as the rivers to the sea; and our souls, which since his eye has enlightened ours have lain in silent adoration, now begin to cry out, "Come, Lord Jesus! O that we were with thee!"

This Advent is certainly followed by the jubilee of Christmas. What will it be, my brethren, when we hear this jubilee sounding in our ears—when we behold him face to face—when we sink down at his feet, touch him with our hands!—and then our souls, in an ecstasy of delight, shout, no more to be silenced, "I have—I have the man Jehovah!" This day shall certainly come. Until then let us sing "Hosanna! Come, Lord Jesus!" Amen.

MOSES' WISH

Exodus xxxiii. 12—18

And Moses said unto the Lord, See, thou sayest unto me, Bring up this people: and thou hast not let me know whom thou wilt send with me. Yet thou hast said, I know thee by name, and thou hast also found grace in my sight. Now therefore, I pray thee, if I have found grace in thy sight, shew me now thy way, that I may know thee, that I may find grace in thy sight; and consider that this nation is thy people. And He said, My presence shall go with thee, and I will give thee rest. And he said unto him, If thy presence go not with me, carry us not up hence. For wherein shall it be known here that I and thy people have found grace in thy sight? Is it not in that thou goest with us? so shall we be separated, I and thy people, from all the people that are upon the face of the earth. And the Lord said unto Moses, I will do this thing also that thou hast spoken; for thou hast found grace in my sight, and I know thee by name. And he said, I beseech thee, shew me thy glory.

If we wish to discover the most glorious moments in the life of the great leader of the people of Israel, where, think ye, ought we to seek them? Many would reply, that the brightest period of his history, is where the Angel of the Covenant appeared to him in the burning bush, and called him forth to become the deliverer of his people; or perhaps, where he performed miracle after miracle with his wonderful rod in the presence of Pharaoh. Others may select that passage in Exodus where the children of Israel passed through the sea on dry ground, the waters being gathered up like a wall on the right hand and on the left; or the destruction of the Amalekites by the efficacy of Moses' arms of prayer. And truly, in each of those scenes his life shines with transcendent splendour; still we doubt much if Moses would have selected any of those moments as the most glorious he had ever experienced. Where then did he enjoy the Tabor hours of his existence? Is it difficult to answer the question? Under the thunder-clouds of the mountain, when it burned with fire. On Sinai and Horeb, when on one side appeared all the terrors of God, Moses stood at the highest point of his glory; for never had the heaven of the new testament been so clearly manifested before him, as here in the awful presence of the Lord; never had the day of the Son of man appeared to his eyes in such clear brightness, and never had he so joyfully realized the words of Eve, "I have the man Jehovah," as in that place, which was at the same time the scene of his bitterest sufferings, and where, overpowered by a terror such as he had never before felt, he broke forth into the cry, "I exceedingly fear and quake!"

The contemplations of to-day are intended to show us how beautifully, notwithstanding the fiery terrors of the mountain, the sunny splendour of Zion and of the gospel illumined his heart. Let us now therefore direct our attention—to the state of Moses' mind—to his prayer—to its gracious acceptance with God—and to the effect of this upon the heart of the petitioner.

I. Moses had left the summit of Mount Sinai, when our history commences; but it does not find him in a cheerful or happy frame of mind. His heart is torn with anguish, and his tumultuous feelings resemble a raging sea. Grief, compassion, fear, anger, and displeasure are heaving his bosom in wild confusion ; no clear rainbow can be discerned above ; and the star of peace, overcast by dark clouds, has entirely disappeared. Most lamentable things had just taken place; the Lord himself had informed the prophet of them while on the mountain : " Go get thee down ; for thy people, which thou broughtest out of the land of Egypt, have corrupted themselves. They have turned aside quickly out of the way which I commanded them ; they have made them a molten calf, and have worshipped it, and have sacrificed thereunto, and said, These be thy gods, O Israel, which have brought thee up out of the land of Egypt. And the Lord said unto Moses, I have seen this people, and, behold, it is a stiff-necked people. Now therefore let me alone, that my wrath may wax hot against them, and that I may consume them." Thus the Lord spoke unto Moses out of the darkness of the mountain. What a thunder-bolt was this to the heart of the faithful prophet! He felt as though these words had levelled him with the dust at his feet. Burning wrath seized him at first ;—but mercy and compassion soon regained the pre-eminence. For Israel's sake he threw himself into the gap, and cried out, " Lord, why doth thy wrath wax hot against thy people which thou hast brought forth out of the land of Egypt with great power, and with a mighty hand? Wherefore should the Egyptians speak, and say, For mischief did he bring them out, to slay them in the mountains, and to consume them from the face of the earth? Turn from thy fierce wrath, and repent of this evil against thy people. Remember Abraham, Isaac and Israel, thy servants, to whom thou swarest by thine own self, and saidst unto them, I will multiply your seed as the stars of heaven; and all this land that I have spoken of will I give unto your seed, and they shall inherit it for ever." Thus said Moses; and lo, continues the history, "the Lord repented of the evil which he thought to do unto his people." As soon as the great lawgiver became certain that Israel was not to be destroyed, he descended from Mount Sinai, with the tables of the law in his hands, in order to convince himself with his own eyes of the terrible sin of his people. But when he approached the camp, and heard from a distance the disgusting shouts and revelry, and the noise of the dancing round the golden calf, it seemed as though he now comprehended all for the first time. His anger waxed hot, and in his zeal he hurled from him the tables of the law, so that they broke into a thousand pieces. Then, full of holy indignation, he rushed into the midst of the insane multitude—took the calf—ground it to powder—and summoning the sons of Levi around him with the cry, "Who is on the Lord's side? Let him come unto me!" commanded them to gird on their swords, fall without mercy on the madmen, and slay them. Three thousand men fell on that day by the avenging swords of the sons of Levi, a sacrifice to their own guilt, and a bloody monument of the justice and fiery indignation of Jehovah. Then said Moses unto the people, "Ye have sinned a great sin: and now I will go up unto the Lord; peradventure I shall make an atonement for your sin." He now re-ascended the mountain, and once more addressing the Lord, uttered here the well-known and ever-memorable words, "Yet now, if thou wilt, forgive their sin; and if not, blot me, I pray thee, out of thy book which thou hast written." Alas! this ardent prayer was answered with a poor consolation. The Lord said unto Moses, "Whosoever hath sinned against me, him will I blot out of my book. Therefore now go, lead the people unto the place of which I have spoken unto thee. Behold, mine angel shall go before thee; nevertheless, in the day when I visit, I will visit their sin upon them." Moses had not expected this answer:—the punishment had only been deferred, and not remitted; and an angel had been promised to guide them instead of Jehovah himself. This was again repeated to him shortly after, and in a manner still more explicit. The Lord said unto Moses, (who now stood for the children of Israel,) "I will send an angel before thee . . . for I will not go up in the midst of thee, for thou art a stiff-necked people; lest I consume thee in the way."

These things had just happened to Moses at the moment when our history commences. Can you wonder now that we should find his mind in a state which more resembles a stormy night upon a raging sea than the calm serenity of a mild spring morning? No, he is not yet composed; his soul is still disquieted within him; and although he once more addresses God in prayer, it seems as if he never before had stood in the presence of Jehovah in a state of such oppression and anguish. "See!" he cries in the bitterness of his heart, "thou sayest unto me, Bring up this people; and thou hast not let me know whom thou wilt send with me!" As he begins to pray, let us remark what a change rapidly comes over him. A dark thunder-cloud threatens us with destruction—when suddenly a mighty storm arises to drive it away; and it seems as though we never behold the heaven above us shine upon our heads more beautifully or more benignantly than at this moment. That which took place in the soul of Moses was exactly similar. A miraculous star rose up during the night which oppressed his heart; a star whose splendour chased the darkness away. A thousand recollections sprang up out of the tempestuous waves of his spirit, in whose soft harmony the discord of his soul died away and was no longer heard. Like David afterwards, who thought during the night upon the music of his harp, he now called to mind by-gone songs of joy. The most beautiful and the most happy moments of his life arrayed themselves in fresh colours before the eyes of his soul. He remembered in what a near relation he stood to his God, and his God to him; and along with this remembrance there arose up within him a light, a freedom, and a joy, against which no sorrow and no grief could have power.

Jehovah had formerly said to him, "I know thee by name!" And as the olive branch had been carried by the dove to Noah, so these words at a happy hour were borne to Moses on the wings of memory. Well did he know all that they comprehended—a salutation of love out of the mouth of God—the affection of a father's heart. It was as much as to say, "Thou art one chosen out of a thousand, protected by my power and cherished by my grace." Yet it said much more than this, for God's words always contain worlds of signification. They resemble the deep and inscrutable heaven of night, which the farther it extends, is the more richly strewed with stars; and the deeper the gaze penetrates, the longer is the eye fixed in astonishment. On another occasion, Jehovah had said to Moses, "Thou hast also found grace in my sight!" And was not this expression like a heavenly archive to the prophet, filled with the most blessed documents? In it there lay the handwriting of God, corroborating his right of citizenship in heaven—an assurance of eternal life, which no gold could purchase—a record of the pardon of his sins, before which all accusers must become dumb—a bond of peace and a passport on the road to his Father's house, against which no hindrance could avail. But who is able to express all that lay contained in it! The two sentences, "I know thee by name," and "Thou hast also found grace in my sight," were as if God had bequeathed to him the whole tenderness of his heart. They arose in the midst of the darkness of his soul, like two angels of peace with balm-branches in their hands; upon which all sorrow and grief disappeared, and the dark oppression which had weighed down his bosom gave place to the most childlike confidence and the most joyful hope.

How happy should we be, my brethren, if at any time of our life's pilgrimage such sentences of God should be addressed to us! It might happen that those assurances of grace with which we are greeted from the lips of God himself should disappear for a time, enveloped in the clouds of doubt and unbelief; but at the right hour they would shine forth in our hearts with benignant lustre, like the bright constellations of heaven; and ere we were aware, restored to all their former beauty, be to us every thing of which in our peculiar circumstances we had need:—torches shining during the night—the sound of heavenly harps in the vale of tears—rocks under our feet supporting us in the deep sea—and secure and beautifully garlanded barks of deliverance coming through the stormy breakers to the aid of our shipwrecked souls. To have those divine words, spoken by the lips of Him who is unchangeable, preserved in the casket of our hearts, is indeed a treasure! Guard it carefully, thou who hast it! and though thy house may be in flames, let it burn; only save this precious document!

II. Moses prays. How joyfully do his words now sound; and what blissful confidence in the friendship and love of God do they express! Listen to the words of his prayer. "See, thou sayest unto me, Bring up this people; and thou hast not let me know whom thou wilt send with me; yet thou hast said, I know thee by name, and thou hast also found grace in my sight. Now therefore, I pray thee, if I have found grace in thy sight, shew me now thy way, that I may know thee, that I may find grace in thy sight; and consider that this nation is thy people!" Excellent prayer, and most worthy of imitation! Thus man must hold God to his word, and rest firmly and unweariedly on his promises of mercy. Hereby he only gives him the honour which belongs to him as a God of truth ; and such a child-like and holy confidence will never meet with refusal. But what is it that Moses most especially desires in this request ? He says, " Thou hast not let me know whom thou wilt send with me." Has not God let him know it ? Has he not three successive times said unto him, that he would send his angel to guide him in his journey over the desert ? Certainly he had done so ; but the idea of this angel seems to have passed through the prophet's mind without finding a resting-place. " What angel ?" thought Moses. An angel was not what he had expected : another guide was in his heart and wishes ; and this other was Christ—Christ the Son of the living God himself!

We are now at the third period of the kingdom of God ; in the days of the Law,—when we behold the promised Mediator reflected as in a mirror in the faith and desire of a sinner, and comprehended in the most vivid manner by the human mind. The star of Jacob now shines so brightly in the heaven of revelation, that even the eye dimmed with tears and weeping for salvation can clearly discern it. The Bible as yet was small, and in a narrow compass ; but not the less numerous and frequent were the lights which it scattered to illuminate the darkness in which the sinner's life was enveloped. Already it contained the promise, that the woman's seed should bruise the serpent's head ;—the all-expressive words of Eve at the birth of Cain, " I have gotten a man from the Lord !" or as we render it, " I have the man Jehovah !"—Lamech's prophetic words at the birth of his son, "This same shall comfort us concerning our work and toil of our hands, because of the ground which the Lord hath cursed;"—and the mighty revelations and promises of the covenant which God made to Noah, so full of comfort and consolation;—all was already contained in the little Bible. Amidst the clouds might be seen the rainbow, like a golden circlet, binding together all Jehovah's assurances of grace, and miraculously sealing to believers the promise of the great Saviour. And what a glorious addition had been made to this little Bible since the days of the patriarchal world, when Father Abraham trod this earthly scene!—a man whose course was marked by new prophetic lights, and whose path shone from the brilliancy of new revelations and promises, as though illuminated by a thousand torches. Like almost all that has been added to the Bible since, they were symbols and pictures of the promised Saviour of the world; and the whole life of the patriarch resembles a wonderful tapestry, through which in a thousand different ways is interwoven the image of Christ, and which is bordered and enclosed by the stars of hope. Call to mind the sacrifice on Mount Moriah—the wonderful visit in the plains of Mamre—the divine promises connected with Isaac—the vision of the heavenly ladder—Jacob's mysterious wrestling with the man who proved to be God in the highest, and the incomparable prophecies which this patriarch uttered on his death-bed. Lo, all this was now comprehended in the Bible; but how greatly was it extended and increased by the promises which Moses himself received from the Lord! He was empowered to say, "The Lord thy God will raise up unto thee a Prophet from the midst of thee, of thy brethren, like unto me; unto him ye shall hearken." By the command of God he raised the holy tabernacle, which by its divine service and symbols pictured to the people in the brightest colours the future covenant. Can we then be surprised if even in those days Christ was known? Then might the words of Paul have been uttered with truth, "But if our gospel be hid, it is hid to them that are lost."

If ye inquire in what form the promised Saviour lived in the faith of Moses and his believing contemporaries, I reply, In that natural form in which the revelations of that period pourtrayed him to the eyes of sinners. To our first parents Christ was manifested as a Hero, who was to annihilate the power of Satan by bruising the serpent's head. Lamech, the lonely pilgrim, amidst an unholy generation, and in a corrupt and melancholy age, beheld him as a Consoler: "This same shall comfort us," he said, "concerning our work and toil." He was represented to Noah, who sailed over the death-bringing waves of the flood, as the Mediator of a new covenant of peace between God and the accursed earth In the promises of the Messiah which were given during the later patriarchal times, but particularly at the burning of Sodom and Gomorrah, he appears, in contrast to the curse and flames of the Almighty's anger as the Messenger of grace and blessing. Now, during the Mosaic period, after the Law which causeth the knowledge of sin had been given, the people regarded the Messiah as a Reconciler—as the Lamb of God bearing the sins of many, and at the same time "putting away sin" in his character of High Priest; while at a later period, after the reign of David, he was pictured in his royal glory.

The Lord Jesus resembles a precious stone which has various points of radiancy, and from which many different lights of consolation and joy proceed. According to the necessity of the circumstances in which we are placed, sometimes one side and sometimes another appears pre-eminently lovely; and there is no situation and no emergency in which we do not find Jesus efficacious in one of his aspects. For example, to the bruised heart we would represent Christ as the Friend of sinners; to the weak and timid soul we would show him as a Hero ready to overcome all their enemies; to the sick and afflicted he is the unwearied Physician; to the maimed and crippled, the tender Nurse; and to those trembling ones, who know not how they are to stand at the judgment-seat of God, we should exhibit him as the Man who is our Righteousness. Thus, if I may so express it, the Heavenly Father turns Christ as a precious stone before the eyes of the people of Israel, according to their necessities; and in the mirror of his revelations makes his colours be reflected, and his lights beam forth, sometimes from one side, sometimes from another. This can be discerned through every period of sacred history; for there is always one side of the image of the Messiah turned towards us, more clearly marked than the others, or bearing a more characteristic stamp; and it is always that which is most suitable to the necessity of the time.

It was a most glorious heaven of prophecy which, star after star, shone forth over Moses and his times. If you desire to know why the prophet wished so ardently that Jehovah should not merely give him an angel for a guide, but one far higher, even the Son of his love; it seems to me that, with tolerable certainty, I can explain it. Moses had already several times beheld this Son; not merely in the mirror of prophecy and allegorical representation, but in an actual and bodily appearance: only once, however, did he behold him in a form and beauty which could for ever refresh his thirsty soul. What a moment was that, when on Mount Horeb, after he had purified the people and every thing in the camp by the blood of sacrifice, he ascended the hill of God with Aaron, Nadab, Abihu, and the seventy elders! Then appeared to them the God of Israel as the Son of Man, beautiful and glorious; a heaven of mercy beaming from his countenance, and his whole appearance full of grace and truth. Under his feet were neither fiery vapours nor thunder-clouds, but a pavement of glittering sapphire, —no terrific lightnings, but all bright and joyful, "like the body of heaven in his clearness." What happiness now flowed through the hearts of Moses and his companions; and what emotions of delight did those enraptured ones experience! Here they beheld the face of God, with every thing away that could inspire terror! Here beamed forth nothing but mercy! Here smiled only benevolence and love! Well might Moses now think in his heart, "Under thy feet the heaven of our lives is blue and clear!" For never before had his soul felt so free and joyous, and so far raised above all oppression and fear. The approach to His splendour injured them not, but only spread around them a paradise of the gentlest peace and the deepest Sabbath-stillness. And after they had beheld this benignant Jehovah, this God of benevolence and love, they fasted not, nor sat trembling in sackcloth and ashes; but they ate and drank, and were joyful, as on a solemn feast-day.

These blessed moments were, without doubt, with the exception of those which we are to contemplate to-day, the most new-testament-like in the whole life of Moses. Never more was the image of this divine Friend and Saviour to be effaced from his memory; and if I mistake not, it was this glorious One, this Calmer of the storm, and Messenger of peace, who now hovered to-day before his soul, and whom he desired in his inmost heart should become his leader and his guide. His whole prayer refers to him; and although he does not expressly state it, it is his guidance he prays for, and that of no other. "If I have found grace in thy sight," he says, "show me now thy way.' Tell me how and by whom thou wilt guide us; not by an angel, O Lord! but give us another leader, "that I may know thee," and experience that thou art my God, and "that I and thy people have found grace in thy sight;" (or in other words 'that the grace which thou hast promised me may actually be realized,') "and consider that this nation is thy people."

III. Moses made a candid and a bold request; for the remembrance of the glorious image of the Mediator whom he had beheld on Mount Horeb, inspired him; and the former promise now recurred to him in all its freshness, "I know thee by name, and thou hast also found grace in my sight;" encouraging him to form the highest hopes. No longer does he say, "I exceedingly fear and quake;" but, exalted far above the thunders of Mount Sinai, he hangs with child-like confidence around the neck of Eternal Majesty; and appears here in such a new-testament and gospel light, that we might suppose he had already sat at the feet of Paul, and that the epistles to the Romans, Galatians, and Hebrews, had already become part of his being. Jehovah understands his servant, and marks well all that is passing through his mind. Will he cast from him this very ardent petitioner, and will he put to shame this child-like confidence? Never, my brethren! Moses' prayer is accepted, and he only hears in the answer of God the echo of his boldest wish.

"My presence shall go with thee," says the Lord, "and I will give thee rest!" What more could Moses desire? "My presence!"—Deeply expressive words! What then is this presence? That of an angel messenger? No. Certainly an angel also was to accompany the people; but only as a ministering spirit, and as the attendant of his general; for another had been appointed to lead the host. Is then the "presence" that of the Eternal Father himself? Still we are wrong, my brethren; for the words "I will not go up with you" may be inferred from the context. The "presence" is that of Him who is the brightness of his Father's glory, and the express image of his person—who in later times said of himself, "He that hath seen me, hath seen the Father;" and of whom the apostle testifies (2 Cor.) that in his face is the knowledge of the glory of God. It is Christ, the Eternal Word, the First-born of every creature; in whom, as the invisible soul is expressed in the countenance of of man, the Eternal Godhead, the inexplicable and distant, becomes near, manifest, and visible; and being seen by human eyes, can be comprehended by the little heart of the worm of the dust.

"My presence?" Wonderful and mysterious expression!—unfathomable to the comprehension as the deep sea; yet sweet to faith as a spring from heaven! The love of our heavenly Father beams out upon us as often as we look into the eyes of Jesus. When Jesus steps towards us with friendly greetings, it is as much as to say, "Lo, here is your God!" And the smile of grace and mercy round his lips, is but the bright reflection of that love with which the Majesty on high encircles us! The Son of Mary is indeed the "presence" of the Father—the living image of the Invisible—and the Manifester in his own person of that which was concealed in the holy of holies. Blessed thought, that it is enough for us if Jesus be our friend, for his favour includes that of the entire Godhead!

The Lord said that his presence should lead the children of Israel to rest; and the prophet found the key to this expression in his own experience; for the manifestation on Mount Horeb had made clear to him and his friends, in what sense the Son of God should bring rest. It was only necessary that He, the all-glorious One, should appear, in order that a Sabbath might dawn, such as their hearts had never before experienced, and that a peace might breathe around them, of which they had previously no conception. No more did they feel within them a consciousness of sin, nor any emotion of timidity or shame. The soul became expanded and clear as the firmament—the heart uplifted by child-like confidence—the feet as if winged to the service of God—the air which surrounded them seemed imbued with the love of Jehovah, and each step which they took was a step over the fields of a new paradise.

IV. Moses' joy at the Divine acceptance of his prayer is unbounded. Listen to his words: how bold and confiding they become! "If thy presence go not with me," he says, "carry us not up hence. For wherein shall it be known that I and thy people have found grace in thy sight? Is it not in that thou goest with us? So shall we be separated, I and thy people, from all the people that are upon the face of the earth."

What boldness there is in the latter sentence! "I and thy people to be separated from all the people that are upon the face of the earth!" But does it not sound vain and presumptuous? Does it not seem at first sight to overstep the bounds of modesty, and to offend the dignity of the house of God? Yet if we felt the same zeal for the honour of Jehovah as glowed in the soul of Moses, we should no longer be surprised by his bold words, for we ourselves should use the same lofty speech. It would make us melancholy to observe in outward life, in action, and character, so little difference visible between us and the children of this world; and we should never cease to cry, "Lord, perform a miracle for thy people; let power from on high flow around us; place us as fiery beacons in the cold and dismal night; and grant that thy church may be beautiful as the moon, or as the morning-dawn; scattering blessings like the sun, yet terrible as the lances of an host; that every one may know whose people we are, and that Thou mayest be glorified and praised by the whole world!" Certainly the prayer was heard; and even on this side the grave, a halo of heavenly brightness casts a mild radiance over the church, dissipating the shadows which envelope it while on earth.

Hear now how the Lord answered the bold request of his servant Moses. Far from putting to shame this courageous petitioner, or damping by reproof the ardour of his soul, it seems as though he added fuel to the flame already in his heart, and poured in new oil to make it burn more brightly. "I will do this thing also that thou hast spoken," says the Lord: and when Moses on hearing this becomes enraptured with joy, he continues, repeating word for word the old assurances of his love: "For thou hast found grace in my sight, and I know thee by name." Moses no longer knows what is happening to him; he feels as though he were transported into the third heaven; he now stands upon a height of new-testament freedom, light, and joy, such as his spirit had never before experienced; and whilst he is in the full enjoyment of the blissfulness of Jehovah, a wish darts into his mind, such as perhaps human heart had never previously formed. He says, "I beseech thee, show me thy glory!" Most astonishing request! Moses! Moses! To what a fearful elevation have thy wishes ascended! One may well inquire, "What is this which he asks?" It is an unheard-of thing! His desires fly on giant-wings. It is as though he said, "Leave thine eternal habitation, thou unsearchable God! Descend in all thy splendour, thy glory, and thy power! Cast aside the veil which envelopes thee! I desire to see thee, O God!—to look upon thee as thou art in the purity of thy existence, and in the brightness of thy beauty and majesty! I will not be terrified, nor cry out with the people, 'Let not God speak with us, lest we die!' Nor yet shall I trembling say, 'Woe is me! for I am undone; because I am a man of unclean lips!' For I know thee, how gracious thou art! I know Him who covers me with his right hand, intercedes with Thee for me, and makes me acceptable in thy sight, Therefore, O Lord, appear! appear! Bow thy heavens and come down; for I thirst after thy presence!"

This is what Moses thought in his heart; and certainly his joy in the presence of Jehovah bore him upwards to a dizzy height. His was a desire which one might expect to have been formed in the soul of a John or a Paul, under the heaven of the new testament; but never to have originated amidst the thunders and fiery flames of Sinai. What a wonderful thing the gospel is, when even a transient glance into the depth of its riches is sufficient to expand the narrow heart of man so as to form such a gigantic wish; and to raise the desires of a worm of the dust to the high point, where the light and enjoyment of the grace of God is no longer sufficient to satisfy him, and he strives to lose himself in the contemplation of the Divinity and all his stupendous majesty!

We are well aware that the bold wish of the prophet could not be entirely granted, "for there shall no man see me and live, saith the Lord;" and these words would have been exemplified on Moses, had Jehovah complied with his request; for the joyful petitioner had imagined himself stronger than he actually was. No! the light of the gospel did not yet shine so brightly before his eyes, that he could bear to gaze upon the unveiled majesty of God; he had not yet looked so deeply into the mysteries of reconciliation, that if God were to appear to him he could abstain from crying out in his terror, "Woe is me! I am undone!" For, notwithstanding all he had already seen, he had not yet beheld the Incarnate God, the God in the manger and on the cross--the Lamb laden with our iniquity, who takes our place at the bar of Divine Justice—who bare the sin of many, and made intercession for the transgressors: He had only been disclosed to him in dark images and faint shadows, but never seen by him in a bodily form, not manifested as that Righteousness which shall be imputed to them that believe. For this reason the Eternal did not unveil himself now in the presence of Moses: had he done so, notwithstanding the peace and joy with which the soul of the prophet was pervaded, he would infallibly have died in the full blaze of the Divine glory.

We, however, to whom has been vouchsafed the unutterable privilege of being born in the noon-day light of the new covenant, stand in a very different position from that of the man on Mount Horeb. We, placed by the manger and by the cross, in the midst of the perfected work of redemption, may with much more confidence utter the bold request, "Shew me thy glory!" If the all-glorious One were actually to shew himself to us as he is, with shouts of joy we should witness his majesty pass by, and cry "Abba, Father!" If the whole splendour of the Godhead were disclosed in our presence, we should feel secure in the wounds of Christ, and sing with the most heart-felt peace and tranquillity the song of the angels, "Holy, holy, holy is the Lord of Hosts! the whole earth is full of his glory!" Did the lightnings of that Holy One constantly flash around us, in whose eyes even heaven itself is not pure, still we should not be alarmed; for, O miracle of miracles! that holiness has become ours in Christ Jesus; and, unveiled, that Righteousness may manifest itself unto us, before which the earth trembles. We need not tremble at the fiery law on the right hand, nor yet at the curses which accompany it. With firm glance we can regard those terrors; and, secure in the obedience of our great Pledge and Redeemer, we can say with rejoicing, "He is near that justifieth me: who will contend with me?"

How happy are we in the full sunshine and radiance of the new covenant! how unutterably blessed in our rights as children! We have no longer aught to fear; for that which was formerly most terrible unto us, is now transformed into grace and mercy. Every wish of our hearts we see crowned in Christ Jesus, far above our highest desires and expectations. One only remains ungratified—but, at a future time, to meet with the fullest and most rapturous satisfaction—and this is, *to behold his glory!* "There shall no man see me," saith the Lord, "and live." We understand this sentence of Jehovah, and therefore wait patiently until the hour shall come. On the wings of blissful expectation we advance to meet it; singing meanwhile with heartfelt melody, "*I rejoice without fear, because I know and believe that God the Almighty regards me with favour. The ground on which I rest is Christ and his blood, the only and eternal source of every blessing. Nothing can condemn me, no judgment terrify me, no misfortune trouble me; because the Saviour that loveth me shelters me in the shadow of his wings!*"

DAVID AND THE MAN OF GOD

2 Samuel vii. 17—27

According to all these words, and according to all this vision, so did Nathan speak unto David. Then went king David in, and sat before the Lord, and he said, Who am I, O Lord God, and what is my house, that thou hast brought me hitherto? And this was yet a small thing in thy sight, O Lord God; but thou hast spoken also of thy servant's house for a great while to come; and is this the manner of man, O Lord God? And what can David say more unto thee? for thou, Lord God, knowest thy servant. For thy word's sake, and according to thine own heart, hast thou done all these great things, to make thy servant know them. Wherefore thou art great, O Lord God: for there is none like thee, neither is there any God beside thee, according to all that we have heard with our ears. And what one nation in the earth is like thy people, even like Israel, whom God went to redeem for a people to himself, and to make him a name, and to do for you great things, and terrible, for thy land, before thy people, which thou redeemest to thee from Egypt, from the nations and their gods? For thou hast confirmed to thyself thy people Israel to be a people unto thee for ever; and thou, Lord, art become their God. And now, O Lord God, the word that thou hast spoken concerning thy servant, and concerning his house, establish it for ever, and do as thou hast said. And let thy name be magnified for ever, saying, The Lord of Hosts is the God over Israel: and let the house of thy servant David be established before thee. For thou, O Lord of Hosts, God of Israel, hast revealed to thy servant, saying, I will build thee an house; therefore hath thy servant found in his heart to pray this prayer unto thee.

In our last discourse, we contemplated the most blessed and glorious hour in the life of the great leader of Israel, the prophet Moses. Let us now consider the moment which most resembles the new-testament dispensation in the history of David. There is no doubt that in the part of Scripture we have read, the royal Psalmist stands at the highest and most glorious point, both of his spiritual and temporal life. He solemnizes the Tabor-hours of his earthly pilgrimage; and whether we look forward or backward, we find no moment in the whole course of his existence equal to this. Let us now regard it more nearly, and contemplate *David's joy in Christ*; directing our attention *to the occasion of it;—to the circumstances attending it;—and to the disclosure of it in his prayer.*

I. The subject of this day's discourse is David, to whom the Scriptures give the most glorious title which mortal can receive—that of "the man after God's own heart." And certainly the soul of David was beautiful, and his character deserving of love. Read his history—peruse his songs—and, in spite of the one black spot in his life, you must confess, that there is scarcely one of the ancient saints in whom the image of God shines forth more clearly and brightly than from this old-testament Cephas. How beautiful is his true and upright character, how glorious his courage, and how brilliant his wisdom! how wonderfully touching his benevolence and magnanimity towards his bitterest enemies! and how unparalleled his condescension and humility!

His principal virtue, however, consists in his child-like faith. "Jehovah," as an old author describes it, "was his fortress, his rock, and his strong tower. When all forsook him, he leaned the more firmly by faith upon him, as though he had actually beheld him. Jehovah was his help in time of need, his light and consolation during the night, and his refuge in adversity. He prayed—believed—hoped, and tarried for him. Though he was sometimes surprised by Satan, and enticed into sin; yet he speedily repented, and was received again into the gracious covenant of God. He never lagged behind, he never gave up his claim to divine mercy. He approached without sacrifice, but in humility and faith, and always regained the heart of Jehovah. Faith made him strong in his weakness, serene in the tempest, cheerful in adversity, unconquerable and at last victorious in times of oppression and distress; and, in short, it made him 'the man after God's own heart.'"

The chapter of to-day describes king David as being now in every point of view at the brightest and most glorious period of his life. He no longer wanders like a hunted deer amidst the lonely cliffs of the deserts of Arabia and Engedi. Saul sleeps in his grave at Jabesh; and David sits upon his throne in royal purple, beloved and supported by the whole nation. After this hero, who never otherwise than at the command of God had girt on his sword, and summoned his warlike hosts,—after *he* had smote the Philistines, and other enemies of his people—annihilating their power at least for a time, and crushing their spirit for farther enterprise—profound peace reigned in the land, and the promises which had been made to the old patriarchs now found their first resting-point and fulfilment. Abraham's seed is like the stars of heaven in multitude, and now possesses the land; Judah is exalted, and couches himself like a lion; and a prince now rules the children of Israel, on whose head not only rests the garland of the victor and the royal crown, but the anointing oil of the Highest; in whose person is united the dignity of a divine prophet with the majesty of a king, and in whose hands Jehovah himself has placed the sceptre. Never did Israel stand at such a height of power and glory as at present; and never was the type of the Israelitish hopes, and of the unparalleled and glorious future for which they tarried, more clearly distinguishable than in the condition and circumstances of the nation at this moment. All the following periods revert to this glorious point in Jewish history; and henceforth He that should come, and that was to govern the people of God and all the nations with a new sceptre, and to make Israel an eternal kingdom, is designated in the Psalms, and in the predictions of the prophets, as the SON OF DAVID—or as another David, of whose dominion there should be no end.

David, with his people, as far as outward circumstances are concerned, now stands at the summit of glory and happiness, and now experiences, in these days of peace and joy, the brightest moments of his spiritual existence. Nothing but deeds of mildness and love mark his path; and his temper and disposition evince an uninterrupted progress in devotion, and joy in his God. His heart burns with zeal for the glory of Jehovah, as though at each moment he were ready to make any sacrifice which the Lord might demand from him; and indeed it is only a few days, or at most weeks since, with holy enthasiasm, he danced with joy before the ark of God. When we behold David to-day, he is sitting alone in one of the royal chambers of his beautiful palace, which he had built upon Mount Zion, and for which Hiram, king of Tyre, had sent him the cedar-wood. He seems buried in thought. What then does he think of? Is his soul lost in the contemplation of the splendour which surrounds him? Has the glory of his riches dazzled his mind? Is his memory wandering amidst images of his past victories and triumphs; or with self-complacency is he viewing himself, lately a shepherd-boy, now surrounded by the insignia of royalty? No, my friends! he is occupied at present with something totally different. Unutterably beautiful yet child-like thoughts are passing through his bosom, and exciting emotions such as are seldom experienced in the atmosphere of a prince's throne. When he looks around on the splendid apartment in which he is sitting, the thought passes through his mind, "Thou, miserable sinner, dwellest in such a palace; whilst the Lord thy God has only a wanderer's tent for his holy tabernacle!" His heart suddenly becomes sad and mournful, and he feels as though he must, without delay, cast aside his splendour, and exchange his palace for the poorest hut in Jerusalem. He can no longer remain at rest; but his whole soul being occupied with this idea, he calls the prophet Nathan, makes known his project, and takes counsel with him how to put it in execution. "See now," says the king, with a countenance in which there is a wonderful blending of joy and sorrow, "I dwell in an house of cedar, but the ark of God dwelleth within curtains!" He need say no more: Nathan already understands the king; he rejoices over his plan; and, convinced that it cannot be otherwise than well-pleasing in the sight of God, thus addresses him, "Go, do all that is in thine heart; for the Lord is with thee." Yet here the holy prophet errs: for though the feeling which originated the project of the king was certainly acceptable in the eyes of God, yet another man, at another period, had been appointed to carry the inspired idea into execution. This man was David's son and successor: for it was Solomon that was destined to erect a temple to the King of Peace. On the following night the word of the Lord came to Nathan, and revealed to him things the most important to his sovereign. The Lord made known to David, through Nathan, that he needed not a house of cedar; and then reminded him of the numerous proofs of grace and love which he had showered upon him from his youth upward. "So shalt thou say unto my servant David," saith Jehovah, "Thus saith the Lord of hosts, I took thee from the sheepcote, from following the sheep, to be ruler over my people, over Israel. And I was with thee whithersoever thou wentest, and have cut off all thine enemies out of thy sight, and have made thee a great name, like unto the name of the great men that are in the earth." God then announced to "the man after his own heart," that he would build him an house; promising him to set up his seed after him, and establish his kingdom. "He shall build an house for my name," saith Jehovah, referring to Solomon, "and I will establish the throne of his kingdom for ever. I will be his Father, and he shall be my son. If he commit iniquity, I will chasten him with the rod of men, and with the stripes of the children of men; but my mercy shall not depart away from him, as I took it from Saul, whom I put away before thee. And thine house and thy kingdom shall be established for ever before thee: thy throne shall be established for ever." This was the divine revelation which Nathan was to repeat to his monarch; containing certainly a prohibition with regard to the proposed building of the temple, but softened by glorious prospects and assurances of grace.

II. Scarcely has Nathan received those divine revelations, than he hastens to impart them to his king. He repeats to him, word for word, what the Lord had said unto him; and it fills the soul of David with such joy, that he feels as though he were raised far above all the cares and anxieties of earth. The king receives the divine intelligence that Jehovah will build a house—For whom?—for me, a poor sinner! Boundless and unheard-of grace! After I am gathered to my fathers, my branches shall still continue to flourish upon Mount Zion. One of my sons shall wield the sceptre. The Lord shall be with him, and he shall build unto Jehovah a temple. He now inquires what is the meaning of the words which the Lord hath spoken: "Thine house and thy kingdom shall be established for ever before thee; thy throne shall be established for ever!" His soul is full of mighty thoughts and anticipations while he asks this question. It seems to him, on a sudden, as though a thousand veils were snatched away, and as though scale after scale fell from his eyes. Now, for the first time, he understands the mighty word of God, and sees into the depth of his mysterious counsels. A golden future opens to his gaze, replete with supernatural glory and beauty. He beholds in spirit another seed than Solomon, and another temple than that built of stone and cedar; he sees another kingdom than that earthly one upon the throne of which he sits; another dominion, another sceptre, and another crown, of which his own in Zion are but feeble types, or dark and miserable shadows. What blessed images does he see, like friendly constellations in the horizon of the coming day!—a rapturous train of lovely forms, which, in festive procession, pass before his soul! He is transported out of himself with wonder and joy, and ere one is aware of his intention, he has risen and quitted his palace. Away he hastens, with agitated mind, and his feet carry him to the summit of Mount Moriah. He rushes to the Holy Tabernacle, and here, in the presence of God, the deeply-moved king prostrates himself before the mercy-seat, and pours out his soul in thanksgiving and prayer.

It is while in this state, that the heaven of the new testament is first opened to him, and that the veil is completely removed from his eyes. It is here he breaks forth in the memorable words, "And is this the manner of man, O Lord God?"—or according to Luther's version, which appears to us the most accurate, "Is this the manner of a Man who is God the Lord?" In other words, "Is this the manifestation and establish ment of the kingdom of the Man who is God the Lord?" In the first book of Chronicles also Luther translates it thus: "The form of a man who is God the Lord in the highest." If this be correct, it is a certain proof that David had not merely a general knowledge of his great Descendant, and of his future kingdom; but that the Saviour had been manifested to his eyes in a wonderful and glorious form. The great mystery of Jehovah's love, in the foundation of an eternal kingdom of peace upon earth, under the mild sceptre of an Incarnate God, was now revealed in extraordinary clearness to the soul of David. His spiritual eyes now behold in all its brilliancy that unsearchable plan of God, by which a Shepherd was to be sent to sinful mankind, to gather them together with the staff of mercy, to bruise their great enemy under his feet, to govern them with love, and to shelter and cover them with the shield of Almighty grace and compassion. All these manifestations of divine mercy are comprised in the sentence, "In the form of a man, who is God the Lord." But, as said before, David does not merely hear this; he sees also—living pictures pass before him; all that is glorious takes form and substance in his eyes—he beholds in spirit the God-man, and he rejoices. The promised One stands so vividly revealed before him, that he feels as though he were touched by his breath. What a wonderful manifestation! A man, and yet not a man! a mortal, and yet illuminated by the rays of eternal splendour! in form like unto himself, but with the countenance of the Almighty Father! a child of clay, and yet the Godhead in his person! his feet resting upon the earth, but his head touching the stars of heaven! the words of man proceeding from his lips, and around him the thunder which makes the universe tremble! kindness and benevolence beaming from his eyes, and at the same time a majesty which constrains every knee to bow. His hands laden with blessings, are extended towards sinners, though at the same time they appoint to the stars their course, and set bounds to the whole universe. Thus David in spirit beholds him; around him the blessed inhabitants of his kingdom are basking in the rays of his mercy; in the midst is the wonderful temple, built of living stones, resounding with jubilees and hosannas; and on its summit the ladder reaching up to heaven, by which the angels of God are descending to the earth. What a beatific vision! Is he awake, or is his enraptured soul merely deluded by happy dreams? Is he in reality enjoying the full and sunny splendour of the new testament; or is it only airy forms which he beholds in the mirror of the future? What a heaven of peace surrounds him! and what a vivid consciousness of the grace and mercy of God is uplifting his heart! In beholding the Incarnate God, he seems to participate already in the joys of heaven; and without doubt it was this manifestation, hovering in his recollection, that caused him to break forth to the music of his harp in those words of rapture, "Thou art fairer than the children of men: grace is poured into thy lips; therefore God hath blessed thee for ever."

O, be ashamed, ye who have not once uttered an hosanna to that Redeemer whose far distant Advent was yet sufficient to transport David with such joy! Remember that this God-man has actually appeared among us; if ye regard Him with indifference and lukewarmness, how the saints of old will condemn you! —they, whose hearts were kindled with the flames of love, when they only beheld him indistinctly and faintly.

Yes! those ancient patriarchs could not contain their astonishment and emotion when merely an obscure shadow of the promised One was traced before their eyes in feeble characters; while ye who have seen him, gaze on his appearance and his divine form as coldly as though ye only beheld a marble statue. *They* were carried upwards on the wings of joy as often as a transient glance into the mysteries of redemption was vouchsafed to them; and *ye*, before whom the secrets of Godhead have been unveiled on every side, scarcely deem them worthy of earnest consideration. Ye grudge even one tear of joy and thankfulness! And yet, would you not be displeased with us were we to accuse you of indifference, and call your heart worldly and stony? Now, for a certainty, we know your thoughts! Ye think, "That which the ancients beheld in Christ, we cannot see in him. We behold the Man; but not him who is God in the highest!" Thus ye seek to excuse your dulness of perception by attributing it to unbelief: Alas! the lies which you utter will not excuse the icy coldness of your heart. Ye say, "I cannot discern God in Christ!" So ye might speak if ye only beheld the Man of Nazareth in the house of the carpenter, or at the table of Martha; but do ye not meet him coming from the grave of Lazarus, and do ye not see him on the stormy waves of the Sea of Tiberias? "The God-man is veiled from my eyes in the form of the son of Mary!" Thus ye might excuse the poverty of your love towards him, had the sacred histories been unknown to you: but ye have read enough to hear distinctly the rustling of the feet of Him, who, though he lay on the bosom of an earthly mother, yet sat from eternity on the throne of majesty and glory.—"His unity with the Father seems to me doubtful!" Perhaps ye are induced to say this, because ye look for the proofs of his divine power in the narrow limits of your own circle; but ye know nothing of those new creatures who daily spring into life by the wonder-working efficacy of his word and Spirit all over the world; and even in the desert wastes of heathenism. "I cannot realize how he still lives and acts!" Yes; so would your indifference strive to justify itself before him, did there exist no other proof of his lively influence than the cold and worldly aspects of our Christians; but ye surely know what is taking place amongst the children of nature in uncivilized life: lions and bears they were but yesterday, while to-day they are lambs and gentle doves: for He is the Ruler of the earth who said, "Behold I make all things new;" "the desert shall rejoice and blossom as the rose;" and "the solitary place shall be glad!" Verily, verily, it is most wonderful folly, and a proof of the soul being dry and withered, when one can hear and see these things, and not be constrained to cry out with Manoah, "*What is thy name, that when thy sayings come to pass we may do thee honour?*"

III. The inexpressibly touching words in which the blessed seer pour out his soul in prayer before Jehovah, show us how he was inspired by the intelligence of the future kingdom, and by the presence of the Man who is God the Lord in the highest. What moved him to make this prayer, is explained in the twenty-seventh verse: "For thou, O Lord of Hosts, God of Israel, hast revealed to thy servant, saying, I will build thee an house; therefore hath thy servant found in his heart to pray this prayer unto thee." How true and how beautiful is this! "As soon as I understood the joyful prophetic intelligence, I took courage: it sounded in my ears like bells on a feast-day, and it appeared to my eyes like a vessel richly laden with encouragement and hope." Thus David relates the history of his prayer; and thus it always happens: there first falls a gentle voice upon the heart, a salutation from above, a sound of promise, and a renewed assurance of grace; at this blessed sight the thoughts which have been scattered, quick as lightning rush together, in order to step into the presence of the Lord; the whole soul, like a beautiful church, is suddenly filled with melodious singing, and the sweet tones of the organ; and like caressing children round the lap of their mother, the desires are directed in love and confidence towards the good Shepherd, and like ivy, clinging to him with their tendrils, remain for ever hanging upon him in tranquillity and peace.

What is now the prayer of the deeply-moved king? Bowed to the dust, and like a lamp about to be extinguished from excess of oil, he cries out, "Who am I

O Lord God?—and what is my house, that thou hast brought me hitherto?" In countless multitudes, the proofs of divine mercy and compassion which have been showered on him from his childhood now pass through his soul. He sees in spirit those bears from whom Jehovah delivered him, and the lions that he tore in pieces by the aid of divine power. Those lovely songs sound in his ears which the Lord taught him on Bethlehem's hills; and he thinks upon the pebble in the sling, which became in his hands like the death-bearing thunder-bolt. He calls to mind the lance of Saul, which would have transfixed him had not Jehovah been his shield and his defence;—his penetrating into the camp of the Philistines, when the Almighty protected him as the apple of his eye;—the assassins who lurked around his house, but whose designs were brought to shame;—the persecutions with which he had been harassed by the envy and hatred of the courtiers and the unjust displeasure of his sovereign, but which could not harm even a hair of his head. He remembers, when in the days of his outlawry, he had often been unable to find a place where to lay his head; how he often suffered want and hunger even unto death, and was exposed to the rage of wild beasts in inhospitable wildernesses;—how he fell as a prisoner into the hands of the heathen, was betrayed by false friends, and was a hundred times on the brink of destruction;—how his Lord and God had not merely drawn him out of every peril in a wonderful and glorious manner, but had also spoken to him in the midst of those dangers and perplexities, comforted and raised up his soul, assured him again and again of his grace and assistance, and at last had exalted *him*, the poor shepherd-boy, and the frail sinner, to sit crowned with glory and honour upon the throne. All this passes rapidly in characters of light before his inmost soul; and well might he then with shame cover his face: "*Who am I, O Lord God*," he cries, "*and what is my house, that thou hast brought me hitherto? And yet this was a small thing in thy sight, O Lord God; but thou hast spoken also of thy servant's house for a great while to come.*"

It is this futurity which David now sees in spirit. "See!" cries out the happy dreamer, "the form of a man who is God the Lord in the highest!" An eternal King of peace! An Incarnate God! And yet this wonderful and glorious One is to be my seed!

The enraptured saint here stops; for tears of joy, of humility, and thankfulness, choke his utterance. Then with broken voice he continues, "*And what can David say more unto thee? for thou, Lord God, knowest thy servant.*" Thou seest his heart, and knowest all that is therein. Scarcely has he spoken these words when a new thought darts into his mind: "The Lord is so good and gracious, and does all those great things for me, not because I am worthy, but that his name my be praised upon earth; for this glorious future has long ago been predicted!" While he is thus thinking, his prayer becomes more ardent and more joyful. "*For thy word's sake*," he continues, "*and according to thine own heart, hast thou done all these great things, to make thy servant know them.*"—*According to thine own heart.*

Here the heart of the Eternal seems to open before him, in all its unutterable compassion, like a mighty ocean of grace and mercy; this fatherly heart, which did not refuse to give his only-beloved Son, but sent him to become a sacrifice for sinners.

According to thine own heart.—"Yes," David would say; "this could only come into Thy heart; only out of one such as thine could such rivers of mercy flow." David's prayer now changes into praise: "*Wherefore, thou art great, O Lord God,*" he cries out, "*for there is none like thee, neither is there any God besides thee, according to all that we have heard with our ears.*"

The royal Psalmist is now filled with a deep and lively sense of his happiness in belonging to such a God; and his soul pours out itself in rejoicings over the blessings which his people enjoy. "*And what one nation in the earth is like thy people, even like Israel, whom God went to redeem for a people to himself, and to make him a name, and to do for you great things, and terrible for thy land, before thy people, which thou redeemest to thee from Egypt, from the nations and their gods?* "*For,*" he continues, becoming ever more joyful in the contemplation of the mercy of the Lord, "*thou hast confirmed to thyself thy people Israel, to be a people unto thee for ever; and thou, Lord, art become their God.*" It seems as if he said, "Think upon this people, O Lord, hold them in thy hands, and preserve them under the shadow of thy wings!" David's enthusiasm rises every moment higher and higher; and what the Lord has said unto him, he desires once more to hear confirmed in all its vividness and clearness No wish lies nearer his heart in this hour of grace than this: "*And now, O Lord God, the word that thou hast spoken concerning thy servant, and concerning his house, establish it for ever, and do as thou hast said.*" Seal it, O Lord, according to thy word: "*And let thy name be magnified for ever, saying, The Lord of hosts is the God over Israel; and let the house of thy servant David be established before thee.*" As if his soul had not already attained the highest point of child-like confidence, he seems to attain it now. "*O Lord God,*" he cries with joy unutterable, "*thou art that God, and thy words be true, and thou hast promised this goodness unto thy servant.*" His heart expands in the presence of Jehovah, and he becomes bold enough to request the present enjoyment of the first-fruits of the promised glory. "*Therefore now let it please thee to bless the house of thy servant, that it may continue for ever before thee; for thou, O Lord God, hast spoken it: and with thy blessing let the house of thy servant be blessed for ever!*"

Thus David prays; raising himself up, by the grace of God in Christ, out of the very depths of humiliation and abasement, to the highest summit of gratitude and joy. First, like a worm of the dust, he crawls to the feet of Jehovah; then, as a lamb which has been often caressed, he advances to his knee; like a young eagle, he now rises on his wings; until at last, like a confiding child, he nestles in the bosom of his heavenly Father, knowing that he may say and ask what he will. How astonishing it is to meet such a gospel spirit amidst the shadows of the old covenant! What thanksgiving and joy for the promise of that King who was to come! and what happiness in the contemplation of that work of reconciliation which was not to take form and substance until after the lapse of a thousand years!

How is it with us now, my brethren? Is the ardently desired kingdom of peace actually in existence? Is the King already come to govern it, whom David and the whole company of ancient saints desired so much to see, and longed so greatly to behold? Yes! that King has come; the heavenly angels on Christmas night announced Him to the shepherds; and his kingdom is now firmly established in this vale of tears Were all those souls assembled together, who have sworn allegiance to the banners of this kingdom; could you behold the peace of God within them, and see the flame of new life from on high ascending upwards; and if all that which formerly was veiled, lay bare and uncovered before your eyes, and you beheld how those souls were shielded, protected, and borne along step by step by the hands of Almighty power and love; if heavenly things had a visible appearance, so that you could perceive how the eye of the heavenly Father watches over, and his heart is yearning day and night for those whom his Son has purchased, and their souls resting on his bosom enlightened by the full sunshine of his love; and if the new Jerusalem could be disclosed to you, and you beheld the garlands and the crowns prepared there for pardoned sinners, and saw those blessed pilgrims, who, casting off the dust of this earth, make their triumphal entry amidst the shouts of the holy angels,—then, indeed, would you say, "The hope of David is fulfilled! the kingdom is come!" All this, however, is still hidden; for we cannot see that kingdom until we are within it. But strive, my brethren! strive, in God's name, to enter it by means of prayer through the gates of repentance and faith; and experience how heaven can actually exist upon earth, in the light of the Holy Spirit, in the lively comprehension of the gracious counsel of Eternal love, and in the enjoyment of the favour of God in Christ Jesus; then will you be able to cry out at the manger, and under the cross, "Lo! this is the form of a Man who is God the Lord in the highest!" Amen.

BETHLEHEM

MICAH V. 2

But thou, Bethlehem Ephratah, though thou be little among the thousands of Judah, yet out of thee shall he come forth unto me that is to be Ruler in Israel; whose goings forth have been from of old, from everlasting.

THE prophet Micah prophesied in Judah seven hundred years before Christ. It was indeed a mournful time; for the kingdom of Israel hovered on the brink of destruction, and the godless character of the realm of Judah had increased to such a degree as to fill the peaceful in the land with the most dismal apprehensions for the future. Micah, by his prophecies, brought those fears to a climax; for frightful things they were which he predicted to the two kingdoms. To the kingdom of Israel he announced its near and entire destruction by the hands of the Syrians; and to the kingdom of Judah he uttered the harsh words, "Therefore shall Zion for your sake be ploughed as a field, and Jerusalem shall become heaps, and the mountain of the house as the high places of the forest." But the more awful the threatening of those thunders which he wielded against the rebellious and apostate ones, the more sweetly sounded the music of the promises with which he consoled and cheered the drooping hearts of the faithful. The very message we have heard to-day may convince us of this. It is a message from God; but at the same time, one which, before it was uttered, must have passed through the heart of the prophet; for it bears witness of a spirit deeply moved and attuned to the tones of Advent. Here is another period of the time preceding Christ, when we hear the joyful chiming of the Advent bells; and here we behold him not merely in the mirror of prophecy, but as received by the faith of believers, and as understood by the human mind. Let us now contemplate this prophecy of Micah more nearly, and direct our attention to the little city of which he speaks; to the expression "*And thou,*" which he uses in addressing it; and to the coming One whom he announces.

I. The text of to-day contains the first prophecy of the Messias in which the name of Bethlehem is mentioned. The birth-place of the expected Saviour had never been known until now; although the deeper and more clear-sighted minds in Israel, had perhaps in some degree anticipated whence the great and long-desired Morning Star was to arise. The nearer the day of his advent approached, the more precise were the prophecies concerning it. In the infancy of our race, the intelligence of that future Saviour who was to bruise the head of Satan was only revealed in general terms. In the times of the patriarchs this Deliverer was more precisely described as a scion of that people who, numerous as the stars of heaven, were to proceed from the root of Abraham. In the days of Moses and the Law the cry resounds to us from the death-bed of

Jacob, "Judah, thou art He!"—thus pointing out to us the tribe from which the Sun of Righteousness should arise. During the government of the Kings, the prophecy attaches itself with still more precision to a single house, for out of the family of David the Ruler was to proceed. Two hundred years later, Isaiah predicted that a virgin of this family should bring forth Emmunuel. Micah then steps forward and names the place of his birth; while, at a still later period, Daniel determines the time when he shall appear. "Seventy weeks," he says—that is to say, seventy times seven years—are determined "to finish the transgression, and to make an end of sins, and to make reconciliation for iniquity, and to bring in everlasting righteousness, and to seal up the vision and prophecy, and to anoint the Most Holy."

There is no place in the world so important to us as Bethlehem, and none which will repay so well a few moments' contemplation. It was situated on a rocky eminence some miles from Jerusalem, where its ruins can be traced even in the present day: "God Almighty established it on the top of the mountains, and exalted it above the hills, that all nations might flow unto it." Vineyards and olive-trees garlanded the eminence on whose summit lay the little city; but the fairest vine flourished within—a vine whose fruit quickens our souls even now. Around Bethlehem rocky cliffs were mingled with fruitful valleys and cultivated fields:—even this seems to me to have a spiritual signification; for some groan with fatigue in approaching it, while others bind the sheaves and sing harvest-songs. In ancient times there was no want of rich pastures for the young lambs, nor yet is there at the present day; but with this difference, that now they are heavenly plants which grow, to nourish the flock of the good Shepherd. When the Star of Bethlehem appeared, the little town had already tarried more than two thousand years in expectation of him. Many remarkable things had, meanwhile, taken place here, which carried their reward to those who could unriddle them; for their hidden kernel was sweet as the gospel of peace.

Bethlehem is first mentioned in the history of the patriarch Jacob; and a lonely grave bore testimony, even in later times, to the melancholy event which took place here. At a short distance from Bethlehem, Rachel brought forth her youngest son; but the pains of death came upon her, and she knew she was about to die. With her last breath she therefore called her new-born babe Benoni, or "the son of my sorrow;" though his father afterwards changed his name into Benjamin, or "the son of my right hand." "And Rachel died," continues the history, "and was buried in the way to Ephrath, which is Bethlehem. And Jacob set a pillar upon her grave; that is the pillar of Rachel's grave unto this day." The symbolical and spiritual signification of this family scene is evident to every eye. In Rachel we behold a picture of all Israel, and recognise their spiritual history. Like her they were dying on the pilgrimage to Bethlehem, although for a space of two thousand years. They hastened, borne along on the wings of ardent desire, towards the cradle of the promised King; but, alas! they remained long on the journey; and many of their sons were named, with tears, Benoni, when they saw that they were not the long-promised Seed whom they never for a moment ceased to expect. "These all died in faith," says Paul, "not having received the promises, but having seen them afar off; and were persuaded of them and embraced them, and confessed that they were strangers and pilgrims on the earth." Thus the tomb of Rachel commenced the list of the burial-places of many thousand others, who in the course of their pilgrimage had been arrested by death ere they had attained the much-desired goal. Alas! many pilgrims in our day, proceeding along the road to Bethlehem, resemble those misty vapours which in the morning hours are seen ascending the mountains; but which, ere they have attained the summit, are dissipated amidst the cliffs and fissures by the noon-day heat. Ye know what the apostle says of those people—"ever learning and never able to come to the knowledge of the truth." And what our Lord also says,—"Many, I say unto you, will seek to enter in," (at the strait gate,) "and shall not be able." Oh that the souls of those people whom we have just described, instead of regarding Christ with indecision and lukewarmness, might be inspired with the resolution of giving themselves up entirely unto the Lord!

After Rachel had slept nearly a thousand years in her tomb at Ephratah, the little town on the mountain again starts into notice; for, owing to a remarkable occurrence, it is placed in a most mysterious and important light. Two women clad in mourning garments come out of a far country to Bethlehem. The elder, Naomi, is by birth a Bethlehemite ; she comes from the land of the Moabites, where she has dwelt for many years with her husband Elimelech and her two sons, having been obliged to take refuge there on account of the famine in their land. But, alas ! now that she is able to return to her beloved country and the home of her youth, she sees herself bereft of her dearest ties. She has buried in a distant land those who made life pleasant to her—with the exception of one, her step-daughter Ruth, like herself a mourning widow ; and who has said to her—" Entreat me not to leave thee—for where thou diest will I die, and there will I be buried—thy people shall be my people, and thy God my God !" What is it that happens now in the neighbourhood of Bethlehem ? The lovely Ruth is industrious, and occupies herself in gleaning the ears of corn after the reapers ; for the two women are poor and in want. Then comes Boaz, the master of the field, " a mighty man of wealth ;" he is pleased with the appearance of the pious and modest Ruth, and takes her to be his wife. All the people in Bethlehem wish them joy, and say,—" The Lord make the woman that is come into thine house like Rachel and like Leah, which two did build the house of Israel ; and do thou worthily in Ephratah, and be praised in Bethlehem." Afterwards, when Ruth bore a son, the women said unto Naomi, without the least idea of what their words betokened, " Blessed be the Lord, which hath not left thee this day without a kinsman, that his name may be famous in Israel!" They prophesied without being conscious of it; for who are the people to whom it is addressed? is it not the family of the Lord Jesus? The son whom Ruth bore was Obed, and Obed was the father of Jesse, and Jesse the father of David, and one of the descendants of David was Mary, the blessed Virgin. How wonderful, that in the fields in the neighbourhood of Bethlehem, by the blessing of Jehovah, the covenant between Boaz and Ruth was concluded! And how remarkable, that the people at that time should say,—"The Lord make the woman that is come into thine house, like Rachel and like Leah, which two did build the house of Israel!" How strange, that the great Prince of peace should have a mother from amidst the heathen! and how gladdening and enlivening, thus to be able to trace the secret government of the Almighty God in histories at first sight the most unlikely! They shew us that for more than a thousand years He was mysteriously employed in preparing with wonderful care for the advent of the future Saviour!

We now leave Bethlehem, but only to return to it after an interval of about a hundred and fifty years. Hark! What sounds so beautifully in the distance as we approach the gates of the little city? It is joyful and heart-enrapturing, like music from another sphere. Yonder, leaning against a rock, stands a youth, ruddy with exercise, and beautiful; around him peaceful flocks are pasturing, and before him rests the harp, whose strings he is touching, and to whose notes he is singing songs of inspiration. As the sun rises out of the sea, he commences his morning hymn—" The heavens declare the glory of God; and the firmament sheweth his handiwork. In them hath he set a tabernacle for the sun; which is as a bridegroom coming out of his chamber, and rejoiceth as a strong man to run a race." When the storm-cloud gathers over his head, he brings out other tones from his lyre, and sings —" O Lord my God, thou art very great; thou art clothed with honour and majesty: who coverest thyself with light as with a garment; who stretchest out the heavens like a curtain; who layeth the beams of his chambers in the waters; who maketh the clouds his chariot; who walketh upon the wings of the wind." Night falls around, and the stars twinkle in the firmament, when the beautiful youth sings his evening song —" O Lord our Lord, how excellent is thy name in all the earth!. When I consider thy heavens, the work of thy fingers, the moon and the stars, which thou hast ordained, what is man, that thou art mindful of him; and the son of man, that thou visitest him?" These are the words which he sings to the music of his harp. Do you not recognise the pious shepherd on Bethlehem's hills? David the beloved is his name. Deep and mysterious tones proceed in the quiet solitude from his sacred lyre; and the sheep and the lambs play around him joyfully. This harper was sent to consecrate by his minstrelsy those silent heights; and his psalms were the prelude to a sweet and immortal song that was to be sung upon those very hills!

David has exchanged the shepherd's crook for the sceptre, and now wears the kingly crown. We must once more return with him to Bethlehem, for in war-like array he enters the field against the Philistines, who have taken possession of his father's city. The king is thirsty from the heat and fatigue of the day, and says to his generals—" Oh that one would give me drink of the water of the well of Bethlehem, which is by the gate!" Upon this, three heroes rush with drawn swords into the camp of the Philistines, draw some of the water from the well of Bethlehem, and bring it to David. The king, however, will not drink it, but pours it out as a drink-offering unto the Lord. This was another important and most significant occurrence. In Bethlehem there was a precious fountain. My brethren, this water flows to the present day, and has water enough to satisfy the whole world; and whosoever drinks of it, in him it becomes a spring of living water flowing unto everlasting life. This spiritual water, like that poured out by the hands of David, flows unto the Lord in prayer and praise, in aspirations and in actions done to his honour; while the three heroes who fetched it from the well of Bethlehem may be compared to a true and living faith, which, armed with the sword of the word, penetrates through all hindrance and opposition, doubt and delay, until it reaches the spring, when it both drinks and procures water for others. May this faith which accompanied David's thirst accompany yours also, ye pilgrims towards Bethlehem; and may your joy over the nativity of our blessed Lord gush forth and flow like the rivers of waters!

II. God had distinguished the town of Bethlehem in

various ways, and thus afforded ample food for conjecture to the deeper spirits among the Israelites. At last, seven hundred years before Christ, the prophet Micah arose, and followed those obscure hints and intimations by a clear and definite prophecy which no one could mistake,—Out of Bethlehem should come forth the Governor that was to rule the people Israel. All the world now knew this, and the faithful were no longer at a loss on what point in the universe to direct their gaze, an object having been provided for the aspirations of their hearts.—"*And thou, Bethlehem!*" Thus begins this wonderful sentence. The words "*And thou!*" are those of the Lord, but Micah utters them; thereby expressing the emotions which are excited in his heart by the divine revelation.

They have a threefold signification. The prophet, by using them, first particularizes the city; secondly, they may be taken as an exclamation of joy and gladness; and thirdly, they express the astonishment and wonder which Micah experiences at the idea, that out of Bethlehem the Governor was to come that should rule the people Israel. It appears to him almost incredible, that out of the insignificant village which Joshua thought unworthy of being reckoned among the cities of Judah, and which was too small to furnish even a thousand men of war to accompany a leader into the field,—that out of this shepherd's hamlet the Saviour of the world, the God-man, the King of kings should come forth. Yet, astonishing though it may appear, Micah's faith is not shaken. No! the thought is pleasant to his heart, and is sweet and consoling to him. Is it not so to you also, my brethren? If there is one among you who takes no pleasure in contemplating the Lord of glory in his mean and lowly form, descending among us in such humility that the poorest worm or the frailest sinner was inspired with courage, and had confidence to approach Him—if there is one among you who loves not to consider Him in this point of view, then he is unfit for the kingdom of heaven. In the pilgrim's weeds which Jesus wore, ye must discern those garments that "smell of myrrh and aloes and cassia;" in his deepest humiliation, the eye of faith must behold his brightest glory; and his garland of thorns must waft a consolation to your souls, such as could proceed from no kingly crown. If this be not so, ye are still far from his kingdom, and the rejoicing over the birth of Jesus can find no response in your hearts.

"*And thou!*"—What joy as well as astonishment and wonder are expressed in those little words! It is the exclamation of rapture and delight! Micah had been threatening his country and his people with terrible things—when suddenly there gleamed through the darkness of the night, a star of hope pointing towards Bethlehem. What then was to happen within Bethlehem's walls? and what did the prophet experience on beholding it? The clouds of sorrow which had gathered over his soul were instantly dispelled as though by a whirlwind. Joy transported him beyond himself; and in his delight he uttered the salutation "*And thou!*" to the little city on the mountains. If rocks could speak, and if solitudes had voices, of how many pious Israelites should we hear, who, since the prophecy of Micah, sat upon the elevations surrounding Bethlehem, unable to withdraw their gaze from the favoured city, and feeling as though in its contemplation all earthly cares and sorrows might well be forgotten! And certainly, my brethren, if we also have not experienced something similar in regarding the birth-place of our Saviour—if we also, in whatever sorrow we may have been plunged, have not at least felt a sensation of joyful hope thrill through our bosoms as often as the name of Bethlehem has been mentioned—then most assuredly we cannot congratulate ourselves that the treasures of Bethlehem are ours. No place in the whole world should be so dear to us as Bethlehem; no town we can think of should move our hearts so wonderfully and powerfully as this. We should rejoice with child-like gladness whenever Bethlehem is mentioned; and if we do not do so, we cannot expect to approach the table of our Lord with a Christmas blessing.

"*And thou!*" are the words of Micah. Bethlehem was already in existence—but where is the Hero—where is the Prince of peace within its gates? and whence is He to come? This is asked—this is whispered in the heart of Micah; and the words "*And thou!*" are but the expression of his ardent longing. After Micah's prophecy, Bethlehem became the object of the desires and aspirations of thousands of warm and devotional hearts; for it was the point of the whole earth which attracted the eyes of the faithful, and the spot on which were centered the hopes of the world.

Even during the captivity of the Israelites in Babylon, while Bethlehem lay deserted and in ruins, it is improbable that it was unfrequented. Its ruins would still be the object of anticipation and faith, and amidst its desolate walls gentle voices would still sing the songs of lamentation and of hope. And now, my brethren, are your souls moved with the same feelings as the holy saints of old? Do you feel the same sensations of joy and rapture? Is Bethlehem the object and the goal of your desires? Is the King that shall come forth out of Ephratah dearer to you than all besides? and if you but possess Him is all else valueless in your eyes? Oh, then, hesitate no longer; but consider yourselves as those for whom the marriage-feast of the Lord has been prepared—as those whom Jesus himself has invited, and who will advance to meet you with salutations of joy and gladness!

III. Who then comes out of Bethlehem? "He shall come forth unto me that is to be ruler in Israel; whose goings forth have been from of old, from everlasting!" Thus we have again before us "*the Man Jehovah*," the Man who is God the Lord in the highest. If the prophecy of Micah appear dark and mysterious, the New Testament throws full light upon it, and accurately determines its signification. In 1 Tim. iii. 16, the greatest of the apostles, referring to the manger in Bethlehem, writes, "*God was manifest in the flesh;*" thus explaining and making intelligible the words of the prophet. "*God*" is the expression of Paul, and Paul knows well what he utters;—for, like the angels that stand before the throne of Jehovah, and who only enter the presence of the Almighty with their faces covered, he would not presume to employ the name of God where he had not the divine permission. He uses the word God as the most definite and comprehensive name by which he could designate the man in whom he revered the Creator of all things, the Fountain of life, and the Ruler of the universe. This God, this glorious One, who dwells in a light to which no one can approach, *He* has appeared, and is manifest in the flesh. He was manifested when by the word of his power at the creation of the world he said, "Let there be light; and there was light." He was manifested when the commandments were thundered forth from Mount Sinai; he was manifested when in a human form he met Abraham, and when he spoke with Moses as a man speaks with his friend. But what was all this when compared with the manifestation of which Paul speaks, and along with Paul, Micah? It brings into connexion two natures as different from each other as heaven and earth. They join together in *one*, God and man. Unheard of combination! Most astonishing alliance, scarcely to be believed! A thousand obstacles seem to lie between, but in a moment they are all overcome. God might have revealed himself in a visible form, amidst lightning splendour in the clouds; or, by a voice from heaven, manifested himself still more clearly to mortals. He might have instructed men by heavenly messengers, or disclosed himself by means of wonders and signs to the blind and deaf throughout the world. Had he willed to appear personally, he might have assumed long ago the form of a holy angel, or taken upon him the unfallen and glorious nature of the first of our species. But no! such was not the Eternal counsel! Not God and angel—not God and Adam—but God and our disorganized nature, were joined together in one! The whole Bible declares to us that it so happened. Oh, unutterable mystery! The Eternal become a creature of time! The Unapproachable, an object which we have seen with our eyes, looked upon, and handled! The Lord of lords, a brother and a relative of miserable sinners! The All-holy One, a partaker of our misery, and a sojourner in our vale of tears! The Disposer of every creature tended by a mortal mother! The Consoler of all affliction, weeping with those that weep, and suffering along with them! The Thunderer amidst the clouds, at whose reproof the heavens tremble—a lisping, stammering child on the bosom of the Virgin! And He who gives life and breath to all, become for our sakes needy and helpless—an infant requiring the hands of men to guide him, and the love of a mother to watch over him! All this is now clear as day; it is the perfection and the crown of the wonders of God! Here we stand upon a height beyond which neither the spirit of man nor of seraph can soar! And this incarnation of God did not take place merely in appearance; it took place in deed and in truth, and is now an historical fact. In order to believe and comprehend it, one must be God himself, or else a simple child; yet, whether it is believed or not, let us still cry Hallelujah! for we know that it has been done!

This God become man is not the Eternal Father himself, but the brightness of his glory, and the express image of his person. Therefore Micah says, "whose goings forth have been from of old, from everlasting;" meaning, out of the essence of the Father. He was from eternity with the Father, distinct from the Father, and yet one with him: the living image of his glory, perfection, and beauty; and therefore the eternal object of his love. And, oh wonder of wonders! it entered into the Father's heart to send this, his only-begotten Son, into our sinful world! The fact of his incarnation seems almost incomprehensible, did not the unutterable compassion of God solve the mystery; for never did the light of the countenance of God shine so benignantly over the benighted earth as in the promise and sending of his beloved Son. The doors of his fatherly heart had never before been so opened to receive us as they now were in Bethlehem; and all the past love which had been shown us since the beginning of the world, seems, in comparison of this, as the first glimmer of the morning dawn to the full blaze of the noon-day sun.

Hitherto a faint and distant prelude had been heard, until at Bethlehem a full burst of harmony proceeded from a thousand voices. And now we may ask the question, What induced the Father to send us his only and well beloved Son? It was enough that he willed to save us. And wherefore did he will to save us? Because he pitied us. Why did he pity us? Because we were lost. Why did the fact that we were lost touch his heart with compassion? Because he loved us. Why did he love us? Because he saw us already in Christ, whom he purposed to send. Why did he behold us in Christ and not in our sins? Because otherwise he must have destroyed us. And why did he not destroy us? Because he did not will it. We now stand at the boundary of all human knowledge and comprehension. This love which made him resolve to give his Son for us, had its origin in himself; and was like the tones of an Æolian harp, which, without being touched by human hand, gives forth sweet melody. But no! this is not a just comparison; there is always a cause for the music of this harp, though it should only be the faintest breath of air playing among its strings. The love of God, on the contrary, was like nothing in this world; for every thing here below has its origin in something, while this kindled of its own accord, and, if I may so speak, was caused by itself. This love we now behold surmounting all those impediments which our sins opposed to its progress—illuminating Bethlehem's night with its sunny splendour—rendering the whole earth bright with its rays, and transforming the death and darkness in which the world has been plunged into happiness and light. This love resembles a mysterious sea,—an unfathomable ocean; you may throw the lead, but here no bottom is to be found. Use telescope after telescope, and still you search for coast and shore in vain; and I think that the view of Adam's paradise, or the heaven which was opened before Stephen, could scarcely be so enrapturing as a glance into this depth of compassion,—into the love of Jehovah's heart;

and I think that to bask in the rays of this love would be far better than to lie in the pool of Bethesda, or to dwell in the tabernacles of Tabor.

"Thou, Bethlehem Ephratah," cries Micah, "out of thee shall he come forth unto me that is to be ruler in Israel!" "*To me*" shall he come forth, says the prophet; and this "*me*" is not merely uttered by Jehovah, in whose name Micah prophesies, but it is an expression from the very heart of the prophet. Micah thus appears to us in the act of raising up a standard of rebellion; he resolves no longer to serve his hereditary lords—Satan, the world, and the flesh; he renounces his allegiance to them, and awaits another Prince, under whose government he will be ruled. It is to his banners he summons you to-day, my brethren! Shake from off your necks the yoke of slavery! Tear your souls away from the grasp of the enemy! Set yourselves in open warfare against Satan, whose chains you now wear; against the world that holds you captive; against sin, that murderous serpent; and against the spirit of this backsliding, antichristian age; and bow the knee to him who comes to you in the name of the Lord of Sabaoth. Bethink yourselves, however, that it is a whole and perfect sacrifice which you must offer up to this Prince; there must be no reservation, or you are unfit to enter his kingdom. Here there is only one question,—"Lord, what dost thou require? Is it my heart? it is here. My body? it is consecrated to Thee. My gold and silver? use it according to thy good pleasure. My temporal happiness? I sacrifice it, if it is thy will. My darling plans? I offer them upon thy altar!" If ye can utter from your hearts language such as this, then the gates of heaven shall be open unto you. Jesus himself inspires us with them;—he himself loosens our tongues. An angel now accosts us on the path with the Christmas salutation, "Behold! I bring you good tidings of great joy!" And we ourselves can rejoice with Micah, and say, "O Bethlehem Ephratah, out of thee shall he come forth unto me that is to be ruler in Israel; whose goings forth have been from of old, from everlasting, who shall be Israel's Lord, Israel's Saviour, and Israel's messenger of peace!" Amen.

THE BLOOD OF SPRINKLING

Exodus xii, 13

And the blood shall be to you for a token upon the houses where ye are; and when I see the blood, I will pass over you, and the plague shall not be upon you to destroy you, when I smite the land of Egypt.

If the choice I have made of to-day's text surprise you, my brethren, I must either believe that you are unaware of the symbolical depth and significancy of the history from which it is selected; or else that you are not acquainted with the aim and object of the Lord's supper, to which it ultimately refers. If that rule of the ancient fathers is to be applied anywhere, "that one should read the Old Testament as though it were written throughout with the blood of Christ;" especially is it applicable to the deliverance of the children of Israel out of Egypt. The opinion of Luther is, that "there is no passage in the whole Bible which may not be compared to a fruit-tree, from which, if one know how to shake it, abundance of refreshing and enlivening fruit will fall down," and this is particularly applicable, where the Scriptures relate how the chosen people cast off the yoke of Pharaoh. Here, all has a deep, symbolical, and mysterious signification, which only finds its explanation in the miracles on Mount Golgotha, and at the cross of Christ. The meditations of to-day will, I trust, convince us of this, if, guided by our text, we contemplate the efficacy of the blood of Christ; and for this purpose let us direct our attention to the houses sprinkled with blood, and to the great passover.

I. The words of our text transport us to the dwellings of the children of Israel in Egypt. Regarding them merely as houses, there is little to be seen; but they have an allegorical significancy, and refer to things the most important and interesting. We ourselves are dwelling-places, and the Scriptures frequently make use of this comparison with regard to us. "Whose house are we," are the words of the Apostle Paul. In another place we are called living temples; and elsewhere we are compared to a city, or a number of habitations, in which there are various denizens. Who does not remember the beautiful allegory of Solomon, in the twelfth chapter of Ecclesiastes, where he compares man to a house, and speaks of the keepers of the house, which are the hands and arms; the grinders, which are the teeth; the windows, which are the eyes; the doors opening to the streets, which are the lips; and so on, following out the comparison. The Scriptures describe those who are regenerated as the abode of God and of his Spirit; while in the others Satan has his portion, for they are dwelling-places of sin, the world, and the flesh. In the unconverted world, as in a city, there are many different species of houses, some having a joyful and a happy exterior, but within nothing but misery and discontent; others having splendid shields and arms emblazoned without, while we find nothing within but low occupations, and foolish if not vicious pursuits taking up the minds of their inhabitants. They are tombs of moral decay, abodes of corruption, and dwelling-places of sin and of death. The Israelitish house, to which our text refers, stands in the utmost danger, for the Lord is about to send his destroying angel to slay the first-born of man and beast. Yet what is this danger, compared with that which threatens us in our natural condition? Do you know the abyss into which Cain fell? or the depths which swallowed up Saul? or the dark thunder-cloud which gathered over the head of Judas? In them you may have some idea of the danger which lurks at your threshold. An adversary is hastening after you, who can destroy, not merely your body, but your soul, in the lowest pit of hell. A death awaits you, such as will remove you, not only from this beautiful earth, but from the presence of God! A judgment is impending over you, such as will cause you not only to weep tears of despair here, but through all eternity. If you pause a moment, you hear the voice from Ebal, thundering forth the words—"Whosoever hath sinned against me, him will I blot out of my book!" Contemplate the rich man in flames and torment, and listen to the frightful sentence of condemnation, "Depart from me, ye cursed, into everlasting fire, prepared for the devil and his angels."

Pause a moment at these words and at this picture; for, as surely as the Lord liveth, you behold here the abyss open before you, which, if a Saviour had not interposed, must infallibly have engulfed you. The Israelitish dwellings, before which we stand in spirit to-day, are certainly severely threatened, but yet by no means lost without remedy. They *can* and *will* escape the judgment which hangs over them; and praise be to God that the same means of escape lie open to us; for while we hear the menance, we hear at the same time the blessed question—"Why will ye die, O house of Israel?" Although we are all deserving of death, yet no one need die who *wills* to save himself; the city of refuge is open to all who choose to flee thither; and what sinner can affirm that he is not included, when he hears the voice calling out—"Come unto me, all ye that labour and are heavy laden, and I will give you rest?" The means which were appointed to save the Israelites are now at our disposal, and life or death depends on ourselves, whether we accept or refuse them. There are not many paths to heaven, although many have been described; not many ways of propitiating the favour of God; and not many doors to our Father's house. Salvation is only to be found in one Person; there is only one name given among men whereby they might be saved, and only one entrance into the ark, for one only is necessary. Mary chose the good, not the better part; *for only one is good!*

By what means, then, were the houses in Egypt saved by blood? "Blood," said the Lord, "shall be to you for a token upon the houses where ye are; and when I see the blood I will pass over you." Most wonderful! And what then preserves us from his anger? It is blood also, and blood only; not the blood of the same Lamb which was made use of then, but the blood of the Lamb of God,—the blood of our great pledge and sacrifice. Search the Scriptures; examine the grounds on which rest the salvation and the happiness of the elect; you will find one thing only, and that is blood. Are they delivered? It is by the blood of the Son of God. Are they free? It is, as Zechariah says, "By the blood of thy covenant I have sent forth thy prisoners out of the pit wherein is no water." Are they redeemed? Then it is not, as Peter testifies, "with corruptible things, as silver and gold, but with the precious blood of Christ, as of a lamb without blemish and without spot." Are they cleansed from sin? John assures us "that the blood of Jesus Christ his Son, cleanseth us from all sin." Are their robes washed? In the Apocalypse it is said, "And have washed their robes, and made them white in the blood of the Lamb." Are they justified? In the epistle to the Romans, they will find that they are "justified by his blood." And Paul assures us in his epistle to the Ephesians, that "ye who sometimes were far off are made nigh by the blood of Christ." Are the elect privileged to enter joyfully into the holy of holies? They are so by the blood of Christ. Do they overcome all things? They overcome by the blood of the Lamb. Do they live? They have life through His blood. Thus all the goodness, grace, and compassion of God is ascribed in his word, to the blood of Christ—the only spring whence it all proceeds. And if a man is lost for ever, and condemned to eternal punishment, the Scriptures know no other cause for it than this—that he has despised the blood of the Son of God, contemned it, and trampled it under foot.

The blood of the Lamb was the only means appointed to the Israelites by God, whereby they might escape the severe affliction which was about to visit the land of Egypt. Yet, although the means were presented to them, their safety was by no means thereby secured: they must make use of it themselves, and that according to the method appointed by Jehovah. What class of persons, think you, my brethren, would make use of those means? Certainly not those who thought in their folly, "We run no danger from the destroying angel." Nor yet those unbelieving ones who said in their hearts, "What efficacy can there be in the blood of a lamb? and how shall this feeble remedy save us?" Such as these would not sprinkle the blood on the door-posts of their houses, and thus neglect the only thing in the whole world which could avail to save them. With justice, therefore, they would be struck by the plague. The others, on the contrary, who knew how to submit their natural reason to the commands of God, and who, fearing the impending judgment, and believing in the saving efficacy of the blood of the Lamb, implicitly followed the commands of God, remained secure, and were saved, in the midst of destruction. We are saved in a similar manner, by the blood of Christ; for it surely and infallibly can deliver those for whom it was shed; but yet those purchased ones must make use of this blood of sprinkling, and appropriate it to themselves. Like Israel, however, we cannot grasp at those means of safety, until we perceive the destruction which surrounds us, the danger which threatens us, and the curse which rests upon us. This, however, is not all: we must have a lively faith in the efficacy of Christ's blood, and believe that, by his death, the dying Lamb washed away all our gigantic guilt: in short, be able, with heart-felt conviction, to say, "For me Christ fulfilled the law, and in my place he stood at the bar of judgment."

Do you experience those feelings? Is your soul fired with an earnest desire to partake in the benefits of Christ's precious blood? Are you ready to give up all for the certainty, that his blood was shed for you? If so, the allegory is now realized in you, of the moment when the believing Israelites hastened with their vessels to catch the blood of their deliverance. My brethren, now is the time;—rest firmly on the atoning sacrifice of the great Mediator; grasp it with sure confidence, as the only and certain ground of your hope; bear it as such constantly in your soul; and whatever blessings you may expect, expect them only for the sake of the blood which drops from the Cross. And what more will you require to do? The only thing which was necessary, you have done. The door-posts of your houses are sprinkled; and henceforward, you may sit in confidence and security under your own vine and fig-tree.

II. "*And when I see the blood*," saith the Lord, "*I will pass over you, and the plague shall not be upon you to destroy you, when I smite the land of Egypt*." Listen to this glorious promise! Listen, and rejoice! Yes, the Almighty keeps his word. The Israelites experienced this, in their blood-besprinkled houses; for the destroying angel passed them over. Yet that which Israel experienced, is but a faint type of the mighty passover in which our dwellings are spared, protected by the blood of Christ. What is it that I behold in spirit? What a murderous train! What a host of terrors! What a banner of death! But I tremble not before them; for I am protected by a bloody bulwark, the merits of my pledge; and harmless to me they must pass over. Other enemies, however, arise—the countless multitude of my sins; and I know they could a thousand times condemn me;—silent and dumb, however, they must pass over, buried in the depths of forgetfulness. The prince of darkness, with his hellish train—unutterably stronger than I am—rises out of the abyss: nevertheless, even to touch me, is eternally forbidden him; and he too must pass over. Next comes Death, that gloomy king of terrors:—he knocks at my gate; but he beholds the blood. The murderous sword falls from his hand, and the destroyer is transformed into the angel of peace. The curse of the Almighty God now threatens me, like fiery flames descending around, and anguish and desolation in its train. Over my head the lightnings are flashing; but "*pass over*," is still the cry. In short, whatever adversary or accuser it may be—whether Moses with the record of my sins, or the judge in my own bosom, or any thing whatever that is terrible or dangerous to man—all, all must pass over, on account of the blood which was shed for me, and which redeems me from death.

In every case the destroying angel passed over those houses in Egypt which were sprinkled with the blood; nevertheless it seems to me, that the people within them must have been in very different situations. I can imagine one of them, when he hears the groans of his dying neighbours, crying out in despair, "How should such miserable means as the blood on my door avail to save me?" Think you that the avenger will pass over this one? It seems to me, *most certainly;* for God, who appoints his path to the destroying angel, looks not at man's weakness or strength of faith, but at the blood on the door-posts. Let us speak, however, to this doubting one. "Dost thou think that the blood has no power? if so, then wash it away from thy door, and see if thou wilt be saved?" What will he reply? "No, no!" he cries out, "for the sake of all this world can offer, I would not do so! Take not away the blood, but leave it still upon my door-posts!" Ye who are faint-hearted and timid in Zion, know well that there is a species of faith which lies concealed even in the midst of doubt. I can well imagine another of the Israelites, in whose heart, as he stands behind the blood-besprinkled door, there arises the anxious question—"If the blood can save him also, for in his life he has been wicked, and pre-eminent among evil doers?" Think you he has reason for asking this question? No, my brethren; if any one is spared, he will be so also. "Foolish man! dost thou imagine that God spares on account of worth or merit? He spares out of loving kindness and mercy, and inquires not who dwells within the house; but only if there be blood upon its door-posts: think of this, and rejoice." I can picture to myself a third, who, when he hears the trumpet of the avenging angel sounding through the streets, in the first moment of consternation, forgets that the protecting blood is also sprinkled upon his door. What happens then? Fear and trembling overwhelm him; his hair stands on end; the chamber resounds with his cry of terror, "I am lost! I am lost!" for he sees only death and destruction before him. Most extraordinary scene! Despair without danger! a cry for assistance whilst in the securest haven! Will the destroyer pass over this one also? Can you doubt for a moment? The blood is on his door-posts, and his trembling and quaking are groundless. I now imagine a fourth. He hears the sound of the destroyer in his neighbourhood, and the whistling through the air of his brandished scythe; but he looks neither upon the angel, nor on the dead bodies of the slain who have fallen his victims, nor upon himself and his own sins; on the contrary, overlooking every other object, he directs his gaze firmly and unchangeably to the blood upon his door; and now he thinks, God the faithful and true, has said, "*The blood shall be to you for a token upon the houses where ye are; and when I see the blood, I will pass over you, and the plague shall not be upon you to destroy you, when I smite the land of Egypt.*" These are his thoughts; and he stands calmly and peacefully by his door, watching the destroying angel, and saying, "Me he cannot harm;" for not even the faintest shadow of fear obscures the serenity of his soul. Would you not wish to participate in the happy state of this fourth Israelite, my brethren? Most assuredly you can do so, if you are serious in your wish, and if it proceed from the deeply-felt necessity of your heart: then, approach with joy the table of the Lord, and come, all ye that are weary and heavy laden, for Christ will give you rest! To this meal ye are welcome, for your hearts have been sprinkled with the saving blood of the Lamb, who was slain for your transgressions.

If we then are convinced of this, what should hinder us abiding henceforward in the houses of peace and tranquillity? Come on, ye adversaries of our souls, and say all that is in your powei against us! So far are we from being afraid of your approach, that we would rather summon you before us, to raise and enliven our cheerfulness, by proving your impotency. Come on, dark majesty of hell! what seekest thou? Satan, God rebuke thee! who will condemn? who can accuse? for here is Christ! Come on, thou king of terrors! thou angel of death! we laugh at thy power. Where now is thy sting, thou disarmed one? thou hast been swallowed up in victory! Moses, herald of the law! man from Sinai and Ebal! step forward with thy tables, and with thy curses! Lo! the anathema falls powerless from thy lips! Sinners and transgressors though we be, we have been washed in the blood of Christ; and he is the fulfiller of the law; whosoever believes on him, is sanctified and made holy. Mine own heart, what hast thou to say against me? Hast thou forgotten the token upon my door? And dare the servant accuse where his king has acquitted? Be at peace, and remember, God is greater than thou, and knoweth all things. Pass over! all ye forms of terror! Pass over with the long register of my sins, with the fiery characters of the law, and with the frightful pictures of hell and of judgment. Ye can never make us tremble. For from behind our besprinkled door-posts, ye only appear to us as a dim procession faintly traced upon the wall, as flitting shadows, or as the airy forms of a dream! We embrace that mighty sacrifice perfected for us through all eternity, and cry out rejoicing, "If God be for us, who can be against us?"

THE NEW CREATURE

2 Cor. v. 14—17

Because we thus judge, that if one died for all, then we are all dead; and that he died for all, that they which live should not henceforth live unto themselves, but unto him which died for them, and rose again. Wherefore henceforth know we no man after the flesh: yea, though we have known Christ after the flesh, yet now henceforth know we him no more. Therefore if any man be in Christ, he is a new creature: old things are passed away; behold all things are become new.

There are many sentences in the holy Scriptures resembling meteors, which, when we take in pieces, such a countless multitude of fiery flames and sparks of every variety of colour proceed from them, as almost to blind our eyes with their glittering brightness. Such a sentence is our text, and it furnishes us with a whole myriad of the most glorious and self-enlivening thoughts; and the more it opens to our gaze, the more does the inexhaustible richness of its contents strike us with astonishment. Indeed we cannot express what glorious and enrapturing things the great apostle describes in those few and simple words! He seems to speak directly out of the holy of holies of the New Testament; and truths are poured into our hearts, which, if realized by sinners, might transform this vale of tears into a paradise. Paul tells us what he beholds in the person of a real Christian; let us, therefore, consider *the point from which he regards the Christian; the light in which the Christian appears to him; and the influence which this contemplation had upon his own life.*

I. We inquire, first, concerning the point from which Paul contemplates and judges the Christian; for we must know it or else his verdict remains to us inexplicable. There are many points of view in which one can behold the followers of Jesus; but people generally mistake, and do not choose the right one; hence it follows that the glory of the children of God is rarely visible to men. For example, let me contemplate thy early life, my brother, and from it decide upon thy character. I see thee a wicked man, worse than a thousand others, and am therefore compelled to form a low estimate with regard to thee. If on the contrary I value thee according to the opinion formed by the world now, my idea of thee is not raised; for the world perhaps describes thee as gloomy and ascetic, a proud pharisee, or an hypocritical despiser of thy brethren. If in furtherance of my object I direct my attention to thy daily words and actions, I probably find thee what is generally considered an honest and respectable member of society; but this is not enough; for thousands of others are so who yet are not Christians. If I look into thy spiritual life, into thy heart, in order to form some opinion concerning thee; perhaps I enter at a wrong time, whilst the storm of temptation is raging; a wild host of doubts and fears are troubling thy soul, and the dim twilight of thy feeble faith barely serves to discover the aspect of things. What then should I say? "I sought to find a silent and holy temple, full of the incense of prayer and praise, and found a raging scene of combat, the gloomy dwelling place of misery and woe!" Should I judge from thine own words, then I behold thee as the chief of sinners, for as such thou hast declared thyself. Let me glide into thy private apartment, in hopes that *there* perhaps a faint glimmer of splendour may surround thee. Alas! in all probability it is here that the last ray of light disappears; for what proofs of thy weakness and unfaithfulness to God do I hear out of thine own lips, and above all, what lifeless, broken, and stammering prayers! You thus see, my brethren, how easily it might happen that even a believing Christian might appear to me in an ordinary and contemptible light, according to the point of view in which I regarded him.

How then did the Apostle contemplate the follower of Jesus? And according to what did he judge the worshipper of the Lamb? Not according to that which he once had been; not according to that which he is at present; not according to the opinion of the world; nor yet to that which the Christian entertains of himself; not according to what he is personally; and much less that which he is to outward eyes. Paul judges the Christian according to what he is in Christ Jesus; and viewing him in this aspect, he beholds a being who inspires him with the deepest astonishment, and at the same time with the most lively joy. In him he discerns the merits of the great pledge, and views him as being represented by the Lord Jesus.

You know what is meant by Jesus standing as his representative. It is the most blessed and glorious thing announced to us in the whole gospel: indeed, without it there would be no gospel, for it is the gospel itself. Christ, in our stead, performed all that was necessary to deliver his people from sin and condemnation. In our name he fulfilled all that was required for our justification and happiness; and that so perfectly and fully, that nothing more was necessary to reconcile us with God. We have nothing more to do than to enjoy the fruit of that which he has done, and with a conscience void of offence, avail ourselves of his merits. In Christ, being our representative, we behold the great article which is unspeakably precious to those who, perceiving their own accursed condition, desire to find a bridge over the abyss, strong enough to resist the shock of all the mountains of ice which may float against it. I am aware there are many among you to whom the glorious doctrine that Christ has performed all that is necessary to our justification, is a cause of offence; because a few cast-aways have perverted it to their own condemnation. On this account you have added so many clauses and explanations, as to say the least, have encumbered and weakened, if not completely altered its meaning. Ye resemble that foolish master of a family, who, in the confusion caused by thieves breaking into his house, threw his most precious furniture out of the window. Ye fools, do what ye please in order to justify yourselves—as for us, we will hold fast this glorious doctrine, and never let it go while we live!

But where does it stand in Scripture? Before your eyes, my brethren. Read! "*Because we thus judge*," writes Paul, "*that if one died for all, then were all dead.*" This is a most important sentence, though at first it may not appear so; and is a strong pillar among the most consoling truths in the whole Bible. "*Because we thus judge*," says Paul, "*We*"—for he speaks in the name of the solemn conclave of the apostles; and truly with Moses and the prophets they constitute here a glorious assembly. The word "we," as Paul makes use of it, betokens more than when it is uttered by the mouth of the most powerful king or emperor. "We thus judge," or in other words, "we declare our conviction—of what? that if one died for all, then were all dead." But how can this be? Is it really so? Supposing a warrior dies for us in the field of combat, must we therefore all die? If my friend cast himself into my burning house, to save my most precious treasure, and perish in the flames, he dies for me; but do I necessarily die also? Assuredly not. Then does not St. Paul speak unintelligibly? No, my brethren, that which he says is full of meaning, and contains a deep and mysterious truth. The difficulty can be explained simply and easily. The word which has been translated in our text "for," has also another meaning, "instead of," which it appears to me ought to have been taken in this case. Translating it therefore, "if one died *instead of all*," we have surely ground for saying, that together with him, or in him, all died. They no longer need to die; for the *one* has taken death upon himself: and in this verse we see such a convincing proof of the doctrine that Christ performed in our stead all that was necessary for our justification, as may well throw every objection to the ground.

"One," says Paul, "died instead of all," and this one is Christ. The expression "to die," as used in the holy Scriptures, signifies, not merely to be removed from this earth, but in another sense, to be removed from the presence of God, on account of our sins; in other words to suffer that curse with which the Eternal has threatened transgressors. It means to be delivered up to the power of sin and Satan, and sent to the abode of the damned. This is the death, which was the consequence of eating the forbidden fruit; for God had said, "In the day that thou eatest thereof, thou shalt surely die!" This is the fearful death to which all of us were justly condemned; but which another underwent in place of us;—a holy, a blameless, and a righteous one. Christ gave himself up for us, or, as is expressed in the verses following our text, was made sin for us. He was judged in our stead, condemned, laden with our curse, delivered up to the power of Satan, forsaken by God, and in agony and trembling subjected to the most ignominious death. All this he did in his people's stead, and in his children's name. How expressive and full of meaning the sentence now appears. "*If one died for all, then were all dead!*" (literally, then all died.) They have all received the wages and the reward which was due to their misdeeds, in the person of their deputy; the cup of bitterness has been drained to the dregs by their crucified Lord; the punishment which they deserved has been borne by him in its fullest extent; and thus they have no longer to fear the righteous anger of their eternal judge. He did not permit only some of their sins to be reckoned to him, but he bore them *all;* and his righteousness, his obedience, and the whole sum of his virtues, were ascribed to his redeemed ones, in most wonderful exchange, and became as their own.

The apostle refers still more explicitly to our death along with Christ, when he continues in the text, "*And that he died for all, that they which live should not henceforth live unto themselves, but unto Him which died for them, and rose again.*" Paul means to say here, that our great Surety has won us; that he has not merely conquered the powers of darkness and of sin, of death and of the world, but that he has conquered, or in other words, saved us from ourselves. Henceforward, in all that you do or think, in all that you care for, or strive to attain, you must have him as your object, and not yourself; and you must no longer regard any thing as your own, but as his. You must be holy, but not holy for yourself; you must be sanctified, but in order to glorify by your walk and conversation, Him who has sanctified you. To enable you to comprehend what I mean, I shall give you an example: there was once a rich man who having saved a child from misery and ruin, thus addressed him. "You know, my son, how I have raised you out of poverty and wretchedness, have provided you with clothes, and by my care have restored you to health and happiness. Now go;

work and be diligent. See that you earn your bread in an honourable manner; a sphere of usefulness is now opening before you; you must only take care that you do not sink once more into the miserable condition in which I found you!" In other words, the rich man says, "My son, henceforward you may live for yourself!" The condition of those who have been purchased with the blood of Christ, would be much more accurately represented, were that rich man to say to the boy, "My son, I have not merely saved thee, but I have adopted thee as my child. All that I have is thine: thy condition is secure; for I will provide for thee all that is necessary to thy happiness; and thou wilt no longer need to care for any thing. Henceforward enjoy thy life; for thy joy is my reward. And if thy affectionate heart prompt thee to hang upon my looks and anticipate my wishes, then let that be the tie which binds us together!"

This, my brethren, is the language of your divine Redeemer unto you; this is your relation to your Saviour. You must live henceforward in him, and no longer in yourselves. You must watch, pray, struggle, wrestle, strive; but above all things discard the unscriptural thought that you thereby become the authors of your own salvation. Christ cared, and still cares for your salvation; in him you are justified, for in the sight of God you are hid in Christ. He washed away your iniquities, he rolled the curse from off your head, he furnished you with a marriage garment for that day, when the King shall come to see his guests! He crucified your old man upon his cross; he slew your enemies, led you away, guarded you, watched and protected you as the apple of his eye. You must no longer care for yourselves; but all that you do henceforward must have reference to Him, and must be done for his honour and praise, for the furtherance of His kingdom, and the glory of His name. Therefore has He died instead of all, "that they which live should not henceforth live unto themselves, but unto Him which died for them, and rose again."

II. We now know the point of view in which the apostle contemplates the Christian; he sees him through the merits of his Redeemer; and judges the citizen of Zion according to what he is in Christ, what Christ does for him, and what he makes him to be. Thus, in the person of a believer, an appearance strikes his gaze, the glory of which enraptures him, and excites in him a transport of joy What are the words in our text? "*If any man be in Christ, he is a new creature: old things are passed away; behold, all things are become new.*"

Let us now consider what the apostle has here in view. It is generally supposed that he speaks of the divine nature, of which the Christian becomes partaker through the wonderful process of regeneration; —of the heavenly mind in the new creature;—of the divine life in those regenerated;—of a new heart, and of holy desires. Nevertheless, I find myself obliged to give the words of the apostle a different interpretation. It is self-evident, that whoever is in Christ must also be spiritually changed and renewed: with the utmost earnestness therefore I would impress on the minds of all, that without holiness no man shall see the Lord. It is indeed matter of astonishment, in what frail skiffs many people venture to encounter the raging waves which encompass them in their last hours: when death is approaching, some console themselves with a verse from a hymn, which they fancy the Lord himself has prompted; others behold in a dream the appearance of Christ Jesus, or perhaps some friendly angels beckoning; and these most ambiguous circumstances form the only ground on which those poor creatures, in spite of their dead and unchanged hearts, reckon themselves children of God, and heirs of the kingdom of heaven. No, my brethren, this is not the true way; regeneration and renewal by the Spirit of Christ are the signs of the Christian. The Red Sea of doubt, timidity, and little faith, in whose shallows so many have been delayed before they could arrive at the promised land, may be passed over; but the Jordan of repentance never can; all must go through it before they can enter Canaan.

In our text, Paul, as we have already said, does not speak of the spiritual life of the true Christian; nor yet of that which the Christian becomes through the transforming grace of Christ: he alludes neither to his regeneration nor sanctification, but to his justification. I have no need to prove this to you: you only require to read our text, in order to be convinced of it. If the apostle had meant to speak of the Christian's spiritual life, or of what we term sanctification, would he have laid', "Old things are passed away," or, in other words, are gone? For do we not always carry the old man about with us? And do we not daily with sorrow experience that he has in no way disappeared, but, alas! is always present with us? We must also observe that Paul, who understood language well, and was able nicely to distinguish differences, does not say, "if Christ be in any man," but, "if any man be in Christ!" thereby expressly showing that he does not consider the Christian according to what he is in himself, but according to what he is in Christ. It is said of a true Christian, he is in Christ; and you know that God himself also hath said that He is in Christ: therefore in Christ are united the two most opposite natures—God in his person taking pleasure in the poor children of dust, and they on their part being enabled to love their heavenly Father by looking upon Him through His Son. In this manner we see the mediatorship of our great High Priest.

Since Paul now regards the Christian in his great Head and Surety, what does he perceive in him? A wonderful form, an enrapturing appearance, now rises suddenly before his eyes in this pilgrim of the earth! Behold an entirely new creature! a being that seems to have descended from another world! Certainly a thing which has been created, but not so easily as Adam was in Paradise, for it has been formed with unutterable labour;—not by the breath of Jehovah, but by the tears and martyrdom of his Son: it started into life, not at the words "Let there be," uttered by its Creator—but, oh miracle of miracles, by His blood and death! The old is passed away! Gone for ever is the gloomy and curse-laden forms of woe, which man inherited from Adam, and which he had made still more hateful by his own transgressions;—gone is the old malediction which rested upon him—the burden of sin which weighed him down—the yoke of Satan which he dragged behind him—the branding of shame on his forehead—his slavish glance towards heaven—and even his old body of death and corruption. All, all has become new: a new righteousness shines around him, more glorious than the first, for it is "the righteousness of God." A new paradise receives him, the paradise of the eternal and fatherly love of God. A new body clothes him—a glorified body, similar to that of his Creator and Redeemer. With new dignity he rises up, for he has become both a priest and a king. He stands in a new relation to God; for he is now a beloved child, well pleasing to his Father. He stands in a new relation to his enemies; for in triumph he has trampled under foot death and Satan, hell and the world. His possessions are new; for the glory of the Son of God is his portion. His resting-place is new; for he reclines in the arms and on the bosom of his heavenly Father. He is newly encompassed; for the angels surround him, and shield him with their wings. His whole existence becomes new; he dies no more, for he has already died and risen again; he is transformed along with Christ into a heavenly being; exalted upon a throne of happiness and triumph, he beholds the desert of his pilgrimage, and the scene of his combat, disappearing far beneath his feet; and sings in peaceful joy, "Hosannah! the eternal heights are my inheritance!"—This is the picture which, shining in all the glory and splendour of victory, passes before the eyes of our Apostle! And whom does Paul behold in this beauty? whom does he discern in this glory? Thee, thee my brother, even although thou art the frailest and most erring among Christians; he sees thee thus stand before him, not in distant futurity, not in that new world which shall be created at the last day, but now, at this very moment, whilst still in thy garb of dust thou art making thy pilgrimage through this vale of tears, and he calls out, rejoicing over thee, "Old things are passed away; behold, all things are become new!" What he perceives is neither an ideal form nor a deceptive phantom, but actual, true, and real. Thou appearest to him that which thou art in Christ—the son of a King, stainless, holy, free, and glorious. Yet it is certain that what thou art in Christ does not now appear to every eye; but does a king cease to be a king because he has for a season laid aside the purple, and, mixing among the people, has assumed the garment of a common citizen? Look for a moment to the twenty-first chapter of Revelation: there it is said, and said before the throne of God, "Behold, I make all things new!" and "the former things are passed away!" What now dost thou behold? New heavens and a new earth, wherein dwelleth righteousness: and upon this new earth, a glorious people, children of the highest, arrayed in dazzling beauty, shining with immortal glory, imperishable garlands on their heads, a royal diadem on their brow, and nothing but triumphal and victorious rejoicings on their lips. There is no death among them any more; for death is swallowed up in victory, and they are become immortal. There is neither sorrow nor crying; all imperfection is passed away, and that which is perfect is come. Is it a new creation which ye perceive in this futurity of glory? No! It is the same as the apostle has already described in our text; only John has, in his Revelation, explained it more fully, and removed the veil which enveloped it. It is that which thou shalt in future become on the great day of the Lord, and which thou art already in Christ. Already art thou sanctified, crowned with glory, and raised high above sin, the world, and death. The perfect man, which with our bodily eyes we shall yet discern in thee, was created eighteen hundred years ago, and completed on the cross by the great Pledge. Therefore it is right that even to-day, on this side the grave, we should rejoice, and cry out with Paul, "Behold a new creature! The old is passed away, and lo! all things are become new!" We do not merely rejoice over thee in hope, as over one who at some future day shall become a king; on the contrary, we rejoice over thee as one already, who has entered into possession of his royal rights, but who will not until to-morrow solemnize the day of his inauguration; and then first, in purple, with crown, sceptre, and all the insignia of royalty, show himself to his people.

III. You have now heard in what light Paul views a true Christian; and he knows that he does not mistake, for he judges according to truth. His contemplation, meanwhile, is not without a powerful influence upon his own character: and he himself describes its operation and effect upon his life, in the words of our text, when he says, "*Wherefore, henceforth know we no man after the flesh; yea, though we have known Christ after the flesh, yet now henceforth know we him no more.*" Deep and most expressive words! which mirror forth the world in a totally new aspect, and which teach us the true mode of viewing Christians in their ideal and glorified character.

After the apostle had comprehended the great mystery, according to which, One having died instead of all, all died in Him, he no longer knew any one after the flesh—neither Christ, nor the brethren, nor himself. What is it that is signified by knowing Christ after the flesh? It means, to know him in the ordinary and human manner of regarding him, as an individual existing altogether apart, and only for himself. That philosopher knows Him only according to the flesh, who laments so pathetically "that such a beautiful manifestation as that of Jesus of Nazareth had only been seen once upon earth!" The historian knows him only according to the flesh, who regards the Son of Mary in the light of his historical importance, and considers him but an extraordinary production of that peculiar age,—having no idea of his mysterious connexion with the invisible church. The moralist knows him only according to the flesh, who admires the blamelessness of his life, and views him in no other relation to Christians than in that of a master to his disciples. No, no: Paul views the Lord Jesus in a totally different light; the eagle eye of his faith has learned to contemplate him in the high, spiritual, and mysterious relation in which he stands to his people, as their Head and Representative, and their Second Adam. Ye say to Christ, "How beautiful thou art!" but Paul says, "How beautiful I am in thee!" Ye say, "Christ was obedient;" but Paul say, "I was obedient in Christ." Ye say, "Christ suffered, died, rose again, and ascended into heaven;" but Paul says, "I suffered in Gethsemane, I died on the cross; the Father beheld me justified on the third day, and transformed me through Christ into a heavenly being." In looking on Christ, ye merely feel your distance from that which is holy: Paul, on the contrary, rejoices at his union with it. Ye say, "Christ sits on high, triumphing;" but Paul says, "I sit on high, and triumph in the person of my Head." Ye look upon Jesus as on a third person; but Paul beholds himself as one with Christ. Ye make a distinction between him and yourselves; but Paul, on the sunny height of gospel illumination, drops all distinction, and believes that he praises himself in praising Jesus. Ye tremble in the presence of perfect holiness and righteousness; but Paul thinks, "Ought I to tremble when I behold my own holiness? for what Jesus is, that are we also!" Thus it is in an entirely new and blessed light that Paul views the great Mediator; and he no longer knows him according to the flesh.

Neither does he know Christians so any more; for it is no longer the question, what they are as viewed in their own persons. He disregards both their natural advantages and failings, and does not even consider their virtues. We, however, are inclined to judge a

Peter, a John, or a Luther, according to the flesh. The first pleases us on account of his amiable and frank, though rash disposition; we are drawn to the second by the depth and tenderness of His docile, yet ardent character; and the third ingratiates himself with us on account of his peculiar union of German boldness with christian piety, and his honourable, straight forward, and manly conduct. Thus the individual talents and virtues of those men seem to account for the pleasure we take in regarding them; and we behold in them what they were by birth and education. The apostle, on the contrary, although far from blind to the peculiar beauties of his subject, views the children of light in another and far higher aspect; and spiritually they appear to him illuminated by a glory, before which the most dazzling traits of their personal character fade away, like the stars of heaven in the splendour of the rising sun. He beholds the church as clad with Christ, the Sun of Righteousness, without spot or stain, holy and blameless, in the presence of God the Father; and thus it is easy for him to regard all the flock of Christ not only with equal love, but to find equal pleasure in contemplating them. In this point of view, he looks with indulgence on the errors and weaknesses of Christians; regarding their sinfulness as appertaining to them no longer, because it died in the person of Christ, and only seeing the new creatures which they have become in Christ Jesus.

Yet who can wonder if he at times chastises the errors of believers with a power and energy, as though he had a rebellious and godless people before his eyes?

He does it in the conviction, that he is not chastising them, but their old sinful nature, which still cleaves to them: for he considers the old Adam as something strange and unbearable, even to themselves; and therefore does not see on what grounds he should spare or deal gently with it. Nevertheless, he at times addresses the same people with a tenderness and mildness, as though he spoke to those who are holy and righteous; for he views them as members of the great Head which is in heaven, or as the bride who, clad in glorious apparel, stands at his right hand. Indeed the whole manner and conversation of the apostle towards the children of the kingdom would remain inexplicable, had we not been assured, that "henceforth know we no man after the flesh." When one comprehends this, all is explained,—the apostle's love, and his chastisement; their nothingness, and yet their glory.

The expression, "no man," in the words of our text, comprehends the apostle also: for Paul no longer knows himself after the flesh; and his object henceforward is not to find himself, or to be found, except in Christ. He does not wish to recognise himself, except in the righteousness of his great Representative; and he therefore knows no longer his natural man. Judge and accuse him as severely as you will, he gives him freely up to your judgment, and joins with you in condemning him. You may put his own virtues and good qualities to shame, yet he values it not; for he looks at the garb of righteousness with which Christ has arrayed him: he is a stranger to the self-righteousness of those who believe that they cannot carefully enough add together the sum of their good works; for his trust rests upon something far higher. On eagles' wings he rises; and it costs him no struggle to despise and hold cheap all that he possesses of his own: for he rejoices in that glory which, independently of himself, he possesses in his pledge. Therefore he no longer lives to himself, like those who think that out of their alms and God-service, they can make a marriage garment, in which they may appear at the great day of the Lord; but he lives in Christ Jesus, in whom he knows himself perfected; and his glory is his great object and interest.

O what a blessed thing it is, in this manner to know neither Christ, nor the brethren, nor even yourself, according to the flesh! How glorious and excellent to know one's self already dead in Christ—in Him risen from the dead, justified, and exalted into a heavenly being! In this condition we enjoy that peace which passeth all understanding; and in it arises the living spring of all true holiness and virtue. O that a breath of the Lord would waft us up also to the clear elevation whence the apostle had such a glorious prospect! This elevation rises above Golgotha, and the bloody cross forms its basis. What a view from its summit! and what a beautiful and enchanting glimpse of heaven! Standing upon it, my brethren, I may bless you with the blessing of the man whose eyes being opened, exclaimed, "He hath not beheld iniquity in Jacob, neither hath he seen perverseness in Israel: the Lord his God is with him, and the shout of a king is among them!" And though it were the frailest among Christians that I beheld, or even did my own form appear before me, from this point of view I should regard it with admiration and astonishment, and, lost in ecstasy, exclaim, "*He is a new creature; old things are passed away: behold, all things are become new!*"

THE MARTYR LAMB

MARK XIV. 65

And some began to spit on him, and to cover his face, and to buffet him, and to say unto him, Prophesy: and the servants did strike him with the palms of their hands.

MOST terrible scene! fit to move a heart of stone! What is it that is happening to our Redeemer? And in what a terrible sense is he become a reproach unto the people, despised and rejected of men! Well might the heart bleed and break when it beholds such a tragedy: and yet when it views it with the eye of faith, it may at the same time sing and rejoice. For here the foundation of our salvation is laid, and out of the martyrdom of the Son of God, the tree of life springs forth unto sinners!

The history which we contemplate to-day, is as significant and important as it is terrible and awful; and is more suitable than almost any other for unveiling the true aim and object of the sufferings of Jesus. Whilst reading it, however, I find myself placed in five alternatives, which I shall proceed to detail. *Either the man described in our narrative is guilty, or Divine providence is a delusion. Either this man is punished, or the whole occurrence is inexplicable. Either He has made ample satisfaction for us, or we are lost for ever. Either we hate sin, or we do not love Jesus. Either no regenerated one can enter heaven, or the condemning power of evil thoughts suggested by Satan has been taken away.*

I. Either the man described in our narrative is guilty, or what has been taught us of Divine providence is a dream and a delusion.

This is our first alternative, and one of these sides of the question we must adopt. Let us now consider the subject of our text; contemplate his situation, and measure his sufferings. Only a few moments before, suborned witnesses had raised up their voices against him, the principal authorities had accused him of blasphemy, and unanimously condemned him to death; and now he had been delivered up to the mercy of the populace, to do with him what they would. Great God! What happens now to the Saviour of Israel! Who can look upon this terrible scene without shuddering, and starting back in terror? A troop of the most debased of men seize upon the helpless One, to wreak their rage upon him, and pour out all their devilish hatred on his devoted head. David trembled at the thought of falling into the hands of men: but here is a greater than David, and more terrible men than the Philistines, before whom the royal Psalmist quaked. Would it not be a terrible thing for us, my brethren, to be exposed to the rage of an infuriated populace? But what are we in comparison to the man in our narrative? The most acute feelings which ever mortal possessed, are, when compared to those of Jesus, like the coarse skin on the hand of a labourer, to the tender and exquisitely transparent filament covering the eye. Ye know how the smallest sin, viewed even from afar, grieved and offended his soul; judge then how the Holy One must have suffered, when the rage of the ungodly overwhelmed him, and he found himself in the hands of the servants of Satan, confounded with the lowest malefactors. They commenced by saluting their innocent victim with the most insulting mockery, and outvied each other in heaping upon him terms of opprobrium. A dagger thrust into the heart is painful, but the sting of scorn is far worse than a blow from the sharpest poinard. Even we experience this; and how much more must the tender soul of our Redeemer have done so? But mere words were not all; for the contemptuous mockery and malicious language soon passed into deeds of hatred. They smote the Man of sorrows on the face, on the back, and on the bosom, some with their hands, and some with reeds; and no just man interposed to drive away the miscreants; no compassionate heart implored for mercy and compassion to the martyr, and no thunderbolt from heaven descended to annihilate the barbarians. Think for a moment, ye who were brought up in civilized society, how ye would have felt this; is it not true that the bodily pain which ye might suffer, would be as nothing in comparison to the agony occasioned by such unworthy and degrading treatment? And now call to mind who is the striken One in our history, and try to realize all he must have suffered.

Let us next inquire who are his tormentors. Men to whom he had stretched out the arms of his love, and to save whom he was about to shed his most precious blood. Think upon this, ye who have felt the wounds which the ingratitude and misapprehension of the world can inflict, and then say, if ye can comprehend how the cords of gentleness and patience were not snapped asunder, when the Martyr Lamb underwent such an accumulation of the most refined bitterness and suffering. The blows, however, which Jesus received, were not the worst part of his treatment; his tormentors went farther—they even spat upon him, like hissing adders giving vent to their venom. Holy Jesus! how didst thou bear this? Pure incarnation of the Godhead! why wast thou plunged in this depth of degradation and woe? And what think ye? Did the spitting upon Jesus conclude his sufferings? No! The fountain of their iniquity was not yet dried up; and they fell upon another mode of torment. They wished to make a jest of his prophetic office; and for this purpose, having bound his eyes, they struck him in the face with their hands, saying, "Prophecy, who is it that smote thee?" In short, they repeated one scene of this kind after another; and blasphemy after blasphemy; for hell took care that their diabolical devices should not be soon exhausted. Meanwhile, I repeat with astonishment, no just man interposed to deliver him, and no destroying thunderbolt descended from heaven!

This then, my brethren, is the terrible scene which we have to contemplate to-day. Now mark me with attention! It seems to me that one whom the gospel hitherto has not mentioned, now appears before us.

You yourselves must judge, however. If one more thinking than the rest had been present at those misdeeds, what would have been his opinion of them? Without doubt he would have said, "Surely, this man, so much abused, must have been a sinner, and must have deserved such a fate!" And if we replied to him, "Not so, he is a just and a holy man," he would contradict us in the most decisive manner, saying, "That cannot be—it is impossible!" And should we now try to make him observe the gentleness, love, and unutterable patience with which the martyred One bears his sufferings, the sceptic would reply, "Let him appear as holy as he pleases, he must surely have committed some secret crime!" Let it be granted that we were at last able to convince him that the object of those tortures was in reality no sinner; but a just man, nay, even a blameless and a perfect one; how then would the stranger express himself? He would say, "Is that man guiltless? and has he fulfilled all that the divine law requires? Then, it is impossible for one to believe henceforward in a divine providence!" This would be his opinion; and, in truth, all the world must agree, that it would be sound and reasonable. For what do we understand by divine providence, unless the eternal rule of an unutterably wise, just, and holy Being, who not only punishes the wicked, and chastises the disobedient, but according both to justice and his promises, exalts and protects the righteous, encircling them with the arms of his tenderness, and making them happy, soul and body? And what then becomes of this holy and righteous governance, if yonder bruised reed is a holy man? And where is divine providence, if not even the smallest guilt can be attached to this martyr? Most true it is, that if in this Jesus we only perceive the righteous and innocent being which he is in his own person, then in our narrative there is a rock, on which the whole doctrine of divine providence suffers shipwreck. Then it is clear that chance rules every thing; that there is no superintendence of eternal righteousness, and no God of wisdom and order! Every thinking being is thus compelled to admit, that either the weight of sin rests upon Jesus, or he must henceforward renounce the blessed and consoling idea of a divine providence. There is no other alternative. And so, my brethren, our history, which we have been contemplating to-day, seems to me to prove this truth, *that Christ bore the burden of our sins;* and surely all that confirms it must be welcome to us, for it is *the gospel of peace.*

II. Either the suffering Jesus is punished by God, or the whole occurrence remains inexplicable. You know of what immense importance it is that the doctrine be firmly established, that Jesus underwent all with which the divine law threatens sinners. A gospel which could promise us mercy, without informing us who was to bear the curse which had rested upon us, never could have tranquillized our minds, and calmed our terrors; for of this I am certain, that I, as a transgressor, deserve death, and not life. The law pronounces against me a sentence of death, and this sentence is irrevocable. The holy and just God must put it into execution, or how otherwise can he remain just and holy? Thus I stand in need of a gospel, which not merely promises me salvation, but which shows me I am acquitted by eternal justice, and not by caprice. And such a gospel we have; for I maintain that the sentence of death under which we lay has been executed in the person of our great representative, who made atonement for our guilt. Our peace of mind, therefore, rests henceforward upon a rock; for the sufferings which Christ underwent, were the punishments of God for our sins: and our curse was laid upon the Lamb who was slain, not merely for us, but in our stead.

The history which we contemplate to-day, clearly proves that the passion of our great Mediator was of this mysterious nature. Regard for a moment the terrific scene; look at the Man of sorrows, and then say if these wonders can be accounted for in any other way than by admitting that Jesus was punished by God for the sins of others. But perhaps you may say, "No! the Father did not punish the Son, he merely tried him!" If so, I appeal to your feelings, and ask if the Almighty could thus have subjected the Beloved of his heart, whose faithfulness and holiness he knew from all eternity, to the utmost extent of disgrace and torture, for no other purpose than to prove and try him? Will you reply, "God did not wish to punish his only-begotten Son, but to purify him?" Then I remind you that nothing can be purified which is not mingled with impure element.

And will you subscribe to the opinion of those who maintain that Christ took upon himself our original sin in order to annihilate it by a conflict with his own flesh? If so, let me ask you how you can make this blasphemous doctrine agree with the words, "The prince of this world cometh, and hath nothing in me:" or, in other words, He finds no point in my character whereby I can be assailed by his temptations. Perhaps you will now say, God did not punish his Son, but only gave us in him an example and pattern to teach us how we should undergo suffering. What! such a gigantic sacrifice in order to attain such a small object! so dear a price for such an unimportant result! No, no, my brethren; regard once more Him that was despised and rejected of men; look at his agonized countenance, his bleeding back, his head crowned with thorns; and listen to the blasphemies and hellish laughter which pierce his very soul; and then yield to the voice of your heart, which calls out in the most earnest manner, "Truly if God had only meant to try his beloved Son, or give him as an example to us, he would have attained his object by very different means, than by subjecting him to the most wanton cruelty and debasement!" Yes, give ear to that inward voice, which tells you that Jesus must have borne the curse of our sins; for in no other point of view can the mystery of his sufferings and of his passion be explained.

Most assuredly, my brethren, it must have been so; and deep and wonderful thoughts must have passed through the soul of our Redeemer at the moment when the wretches who surrounded him cried out, mocking, "Prophesy, who it is that smote thee?" Alas! he knew well who it was that smote him: the Father himself smote him, although humanly speaking, it was with a bleeding heart. The words, "Cursed be every one!" were in him fulfilled: he suffered what was due to our sins; and in his passion he was the man of whom it was written in the Prophets, "Awake, O sword, against my shepherd, and against the man that is my fellow, saith the Lord of hosts; smite the shepherd, and the sheep shall be scattered."

III. Either the Sufferer in our text made ample satisfaction for us to Divine Justice, or we are lost beyond redemption. This is most vividly impressed upon our minds, when we regard the tormentors by whom the Redeemer is surrounded. Think you that they may venture to hope for heaven and happiness? The question appears, at first sight, almost absurd; but I repeat it. Tell me, then, what think ye? With one voice I hear you reply, "If those sinners can ever be justified, and enjoy the love of God and the blessedness of heaven, then we no longer pretend to know what God and heaven are! God must annihilate them, and pursue them with the thunders of his vengeance; or else his throne is no longer established in righteousness!" You are right, my brethren; he must condemn them; he must, if he is just and holy. But are you aware who the people are, whom you thus adjudge to be worthy of death? My brethren, I entreat you to believe me, they are our representatives. Perhaps I may fail to convince you; but in that case a greater will demonstrate it—the Invisible, of whom it stands written, that "when he is come, he will reprove the world of sin." John xvi. 18. If this be true, it is evident that we are by nature no better than the miscreants who wreaked their evil passions on our unoffending Lord; for in our own bodies we carry the germ and seed of that leprosy of sin which broke out so terriffically in them. The same brand of hatred, bitterness, and enmity to Christ, has been impressed on our houses, and on our very limbs; though in our persons perhaps the volcanic crater may only smoke, while in theirs it burst forth into flames. No, you behold nothing strange or foreign to yourselves in those servants of Satan; you see only the old Adam unveiled. That poisonous plant whose roots are visible in yourselves, in them has attained the ripeness of summer. But God looks into the heart, and in his eyes ye stand on an equality with those sinners. And now, my brethren, I hold you to your word, and judge you from your own mouths. In holy zeal you have cried out, "If God be just, those evil doers can expect nothing but condemnation!" You thus pronounced your own sentence, for in reality you resemble them. "Yes," I hear you repeat, "if it can be proved that we are no better than those miscreants, God must cast us from his presence, or —." Now what is this *or?*— "or another must suffer in our place, and thus satisfy the Divine Justice." Yes, my brethren, ye have spoken truly; and the scene of moral corruption which we contemplate to day, forces us to exclaim, "Ample satisfaction must have been made for our sins, or we are lost beyond redemption!"

IV. Either we are at variance with sin, and hate it; or we do not love Jesus! And to this conclusion our text compels us. Ye know already what a tempest of shame and woe broke over the head of our Lord Jesus; and never had ye beheld the Holy One in such fearful circumstances, and never had he undergone such unutterable agony and shame, had love not impelled him to suffer in our stead the decree of Eternal Justice. He reaped the harvest of our sins; he suffered from the flame which our misdeeds had kindled; and the sword struck him which our transgressions had drawn out of its sheath. In a word, the wickedness which ye have committed, and which is implanted in your very nature, is the true and only cause of our sufferings which our great Pledge underwent. Reflect upon this; and then tell me how you feel towards that which made your Saviour bleed! Do you still embrace sin, that murderer of the Lord Jesus, instead of detesting it with all the fervour of your natures? Do you still cherish it, instead of flying its presence, and swearing eternal hatred against it? If you do so, cease henceforward to assert that you love the Lord Jesus. You could as little persuade us of the fact, as a young prince could of his love to his father, who, on his ascent to the throne, should choose his parent's murderers to be his friends and ministers, instead of bringing them to judgment. Yes, he that truly loves the Lord Jesus, will find in a scene like that which we contemplate to-day, an additional reason to hate, and struggle with sin. No longer will he love it; his friendship for it is for ever snapped asunder; and from the bottom of his heart will he join with us in saying, "Either thou must hate sin, or thou canst not love the Lord Jesus."

V. I am aware there are many souls grievously tempted in the midst of us; and for their sakes I repeat, "Either no regenerated one can enter heaven, or the condemning power of evil, suggested by Satan, has been taken away. Why was our Saviour condemned to death? He had blasphemed God, said his judges; as such, too much could not be done to him, and the ignominious treatment to which he was subjected, was only suited to his transgressions. And lo! in the scene which we contemplate to-day, he stands as a blasphemer of God, not merely before a human tribunal, but before the judgment-seat of Jehovah. He now atones by this depth of infamy for the thousand impieties which we have uttered against his Father. Our blasphemies weigh down his soul, and for our sakes, in pursuance of the divine sentence, he is chastised by a fearful rod. Yes, it is a mysterious fate which thus tramples him in the dust of the streets, and treats him like the off-scourings of humanity: eternal and inexorable justice demands it to be so. You thus see how severely the Holy of holies punishes the desecration of his name, and what a measure of anger and vengeance repays it. Nothing rouses his indignation more than this transgression; and, indeed, all who contemplate the subject, must be apt to fall into the terrible idea, that even regenerated people are not exempt from the danger of being lost for ever, on account of this sin. You ask Wherefore? Does nothing come into the hearts of the servants of God which may be termed "blasphemous thoughts?" Are their souls never assailed with unworthy representations and images of God and divine things? We must admit indeed that regenerated persons are those whom Satan chiefly assails with these his fiery arrows; and it is amongst them that we so frequently hear the lamentation, that things are suggested to their minds, which, if they were uttered, would cause us to shudder with horror. Every Christian has experienced this, some in a greater, others in a less degree; and when he reads the history in our text, which exemplifies in such a fearful manner the anger of God at this species of sin, well may he pause and cry out, "Either no regenerated one can enter heaven, or the condemning power of evil thoughts suggested by Satan has been taken away!" And certainly the latter has been the case.

The tragic scene before us at present, affords us this consolation; for here the Redeemer makes atonement for the blasphemous thoughts of his people, and takes upon himself all the sin we have committed in dishonouring Jehovah. Therefore, ye sorely tempted souls, engrave this history on the walls of your chambers; hang it as an amulet round your necks; and as often as the fiery arrows whistle past, and a hateful train of thoughts in wild confusion assails your heart, direct your gaze through the midst of this tumult, to the tranquil picture of your Redeemer's passion; and take refuge in the blessed conviction, that those evil suggestions, the weight of which is now overpowering you, have lost their power to condemn—no longer can estrange you from the presence of God, nor yet lessen the love of the Eternal towards you; but on the contrary, must contribute like all else to your salvation, for Jesus has taken their evil consequences upon himself.

There is a sixth alternative suggested by this subject, which I must mention before concluding. Either in the contemplation of this subject, our softened hearts must ejaculate with the apostle, "Let us go forth, therefore, unto him, without the camp, bearing his reproach!" or else we cannot be Jesus' friends. Truly the man who, after viewing the scene of his martyrdom, can desire to be honoured and regarded by that world which trampled his Lord under foot, need not attempt to persuade us that this Lord is dear unto him. True love for Jesus would rather desire his crown of thorns than a garland of victory; and would rather suffer shame on his account, than receive the empty fame and praise of worldlings; for to it the world is crucified along with Christ. Yet it by no means throws itself in the way of the hatred and scorn of enemies to the cross; although it would rather seek than depart from the right course in order to avoid them. Reflect upon this, ye Nicodemuses, and be not astonished if we think but little of your love towards our Saviour, as long as you do not, like Moses, esteem "the reproach of Christ greater riches than the treasures in Egypt." Ye must first, in loud and decisive terms, cast aside for ever the gold and purple chains of Belshazzar, and with holy boldness place yourselves in the ranks of the despised and persecuted Jew. Then shall we begin to esteem you, find pleasure in contemplating your characters, and believe henceforward in your love towards our crucified Master!

THE GREAT EXCHANGE

LUKE XXIII. 20—25

Pilate, therefore, willing to release Jesus, spake again to them. But they cried, saying, Crucify him, crucify him! And he said unto them the third time, Why, what evil hath he done? I have found no cause of death in him; I will therefore chastise him, and let him go. And they were instant with loud voices, requiring that he might be crucified; and the voices of them and of the chief priests prevailed. And Pilate gave sentence, that it should be as they required. And he released unto them him that for sedition and murder was cast into prison, whom they had desired; but he delivered Jesus to their will.

THIS is a most remarkable and important history, in which each single trait may be regarded as a deep and most significant hieroglyphic. And, certainly, neither the Roman governor nor the Jews had any idea of the mysterious and allegorical part they were here performing. They acted according to what they supposed their own interest, each one pursuing his peculiar object: but the Almighty grasped the threads of their apparently free actions, and so twisted and interwove them, that, before they were aware, an historical web was formed, whose signs and characters depict to our eyes the greatest and most blessed mystery of the gospel—the high-priestly intercession of Jesus Christ.

He who has not yet comprehended this mystery, let him hasten to study the wonderful picture which we are contemplating to-day ; wonderful, because delineated by no mortal hand.

"*And Pilate gave sentence that it should be as they required.*" These words in our text we shall most especially consider, because they describe the most important moment in the whole scene, and point out the theme to which we are about to dedicate our present contemplation :—" The condemnation of our great Pledge in his people's stead." Let us now direct our attention to this condemnation, to its mighty consequences, and to the enjoyment and appropriation of its fruits.

I. We stand before the judgment-seat of the Roman governor, where a terrible scene is just taking place. The tumult has reached its height, and the fiery sea of human passion, whose waves are dashing against the tribunal, now displays its utmost terrors. Pilate has just cried a second time to the people, " I find no fault in this man !" but this only adds oil to their wrath and hatred. The more earnestly he exerts himself to save the accused, the more terrible and satanic becomes the cry of the raging multitude, " Crucify him ! crucify him !" One stifles his awakening conscience, another refuses to listen to the voice of compassion which is beginning to whisper in his bosom, and a third will not give ear to the mysterious warnings which are momentarily repeated. Many feel in their hearts, " Pilate is right, and the man is guiltless !" Others say to themselves, " He deserves a better fate than what we are preparing for him!" And some feel already the sting of that horrible imprecation which they have drawn down upon their heads—" His blood be on us and on our children!" But these better feelings are soon stifled, for their consciences are deadened, and he is doomed to be offered a sacrifice to their hatred. A thousand voices now shriek wildly together, "Crucify him! crucify him!" The high priests join with the people—and men, women, and children, all are unanimous in desiring his death. Pilate now asks, "What evil hath he done?" and repeats, "I have found no cause of death in him; I will therefore chastise him, and let him go!" But the storm of their evil passions here breaks loose again, and, "Away with him! away with him!" is thundered from every side: "To the cross with the rebel and blasphemer of God! Release unto us Barabbas, and let Jesus bleed and die!" Pilate once more strives to interpose; he does it again and again; but in vain: his voice is unheard amidst the roars of the populace. His firmness gives way, and he yields to the solicitations of the infuriated rabble: he condemns Jesus to be crucified, and the murderer he sets at liberty.

This is the scene which we contemplate to-day; but there is a higher point of view in which we must regard the narrative of our Redeemer's passion, particularly his trial before a court of justice. Ye know that what outwardly takes place is but the symbolical representation of a far higher criminal process between Christ and the Eternal Father. The cry of "Crucify him! crucify him!" is the repetition of a sound which is heard beyond the clouds; and in the sentence of death which Pilate, along with the high priests and the Jews, pronounced against Jesus, there lies another and far more terrible one enveloped—the sentence of death pronounced by the Ruler of the world upon his beloved Son! Are you astonished, my brethren, at what I have been saying? If so, accompany me, I entreat you, through the following observations.

In the first place, call to mind that we are not alone in this world; for there is a God that surrounds us, and there is an Eternal Majesty upon the throne. Remember that we are not by ourselves upon the earth, for our fellow-subjects exist on every side. We live in a kingdom governed by God, and it is not the flag of a republic, far less of anarchy, which is suspended above us from the clouds. It is the flag of monarchy; the banner of an all-glorious and righteous King. Either no God exists, or else God is a God of order, justice, and holiness: a God that hates the wicked, punishes transgression, and, cursing the sin along with the sinner, casts them both from his presence. The Disposer of the universe has his laws, to which he keeps; his court of justice, where he brings guilt to light; his day of trial, when he passes sentence; and his book, according to whose irrevocable articles he decides. For transgressors he has his chains and his prisons; his cells for confinement, and his scaffold; his reapers at the last day, as well as his executioners, Satan and his host. Thus there is a tribunal behind the clouds, which is represented and mirrored in the forms of earthly justice. "The Lord shall endure for ever; he hath prepared his throne for judgment; and he shall judge the world in righteousness, he shall minister judgment to the people in uprightness." "Righteousness and judgment are the habitation of his throne." "The Lord is known by the judgment which he executeth: the wicked is snared in the work of his own hands."

This court of judgment concerns us all, my brethren —all without exception. "For we must all," says the apostle Paul, "appear before the judgment-seat of Christ, that every one may receive the things done in his body, according to that he hath done, whether it be good or bad." But who will be able to stand before this judgment-seat, who has felt even the least inclination to sin? And who can promise himself a favourable sentence, from the court which judges according to the maxim, "Whosoever shall keep the whole law, and yet offend in one point, he is guilty of all?" My brethren, our cause seems in great danger before this tribunal: and why do I say in danger? because, apart from Christ, there is nothing more certain than that it will be irretrievably lost. There are many men, who, when they behold this state of things, hasten to anticipate the condemnation of God by humble self-accusation. But this will not do. Many have entirely banished the idea of eternal justice from their souls, and pronounce sentence on themselves. But woe to these rebels! Others who feel guilty, and seem to stand already before the bar of that awful tribunal, take refuge in lies, and seek to make excuses. Some resemble criminals pursued by warrants of the law; they know the danger in which they stand, and look for safety in flight; or seek hiding-places amidst the noise and bustle of life. Others are evil-doers, who have long remained undiscovered; but to whom some passer-by having cried out, "We know you!" a heavy misgiving, and a dull sense of insecurity, has ever since weighed down their souls. Many hasten calmly and peacefully to meet the judgment; because they do not measure themselves according to the law by which they shall be measured above, but according to a law of their own. Thus, there are different ways in which men prepare themselves for the awful tribunal of Almighty God: but the day will come when they shall all appear alike; when the fugitives shall be caught, the liars confounded, and the hidden ones brought to light. Then we shall see all assembled before *one* throne, in the presence of *one* Judge, and standing round *one* open book: then every veil and every mask shall fall from our faces; each shall behold his own life in the light of truth; and each shall receive his last and irrevocable sentence, which decides his fate for ever.

Every being in existence, my brethren, who has any thing to say against us, is now permitted by God to appear before his throne. No matter who it may be that accuses us, God will listen to them; for the Eternal will appear in righteousness unto all his creatures, and not the faintest suspicion of unlawful partiality will attach to him. The lowest demon, as well as the most glorious seraph, will have it in his power to accuse us before his awful throne: and should any one succeed in substantiating our guilt, God has sworn to punish us according to our deserts, and the utmost rigour of the law; not only in presence of our accuser, but of the whole assembled world. Woe unto us, if there be any one with a well-founded complaint against us! Woe unto us, though there should only be a single voice, and that the most insignificant in heaven or on earth, that can with truth accuse us! Even on their account, the holy and just One would condemn us! Let us consider this, and then judge in what a state we find ourselves by nature. Perhaps ye may think, however, that nothing exists in the world able to appear against us with well-founded accusations. Alas, my brethren! there are accusing voices in all places, and on every side; voices against us both in earth and heaven; accusers from the circle of the living, and from the tombs of the dead; condemning voices in hell, and condemning voices even in our own bosoms.

But, above all, there is the law: "Do not think that I will accuse you to the Father," said our Saviour; "there is one that accuseth you, even Moses." His ten commandments are so many witnesses against us, and so many accusers. Not one of them has seen its demands fulfilled by us; not one of them can give any other testimony than that we have trampled it under foot. Like ten armed men, they approach against us; like ten ministers of vengeance, they drag us forward with wild curses. Not one of them has compassion; not one of them says, "The others have sufficiently accused him, I will therefore be silent!" No one troubles himself about another; but they all rush upon us, like a concourse of creditors on their debtors: each one grasps what he finds, only trying to indemnify himself. They all seek their rights, and they all narrate our guilt; they join in summoning us before the tribunal of heaven, and demanding satisfaction for the profanation which they have suffered; and they are all bent on our entire and eternal rejection. Our own conscience now joins in the general accusation, and ranges itself beside Moses. I am aware that in many of us it is still asleep; but look ye to it, my brethren, for it is a sleeping lion. I know that there are people to whom it has never caused a pang; but let these beware, for they carry a viper in their bosoms, which though it seem to be powerless, is only slumbering; and sooner or later, will awake to strangle them. There are some to whom their conscience, being led astray, bears an approving testimony: but, alas! there comes an hour when the deceiver will avenge himself! In others, it has already begun to murmur indistinctly a faint accusation: but this is not enough, and soon the murmur in their hearts becomes a cry louder than thunder, pealing in their ears, "Thou art a sinner!—a child of death—that is accursed by God!"

In the ranks of our accusers, stand also the angels of peace; these pure and holy beings sigh over our forgetfulness of God; and alas! what an accusation against us there is even in those sighs! Zealous for the honour of Jehovah, they are horrified at the depth of our fall, and at our spiritual corruption; and this very horror calls upon God to condemn and reject us! Even if those blessed spirits were silent with regard to our misdeeds, there is *one* who will not be silent, and whose interest lies in accusing us; he knows us not less than the blessed angels; for he was present when all our sins were committed. He it is that "hath blinded the minds of them which believe not, lest the light of the glorious gospel of Christ, who is the image of God, should shine unto them." Surely ye know whom I mean; it is Satan, the god of this world, the accuser of the brethren, "which accused them before our God day and night." Think not that God will refuse to hear his voice; for the Scripture teaches us the contrary. The Eternal has willed that the prince of hell, with his angels of darkness, should pay him homage, and along with the rest of creation, acknowledge that he is just. For this reason he will not refuse him an audience; on the contrary, he will listen to his accusations, examine into their truth, and if they are well grounded, admit them. If, however, there were no such being as Satan in existence, there would still be no want of accusers. Our enemies, whose presence we avoid, accuse us; even those weak ones accuse us, whom, intentionally or unintentionally, we have led astray; the poor, against whom we have closed our hearts; the widows and orphans, whose tearful eyes we have not dried; the instructors to whose voices we would not listen; nay, although silently, even our own sons and daughters, to whom we may not have acted as we ought. Our whole life bears witness against us before the throne of God;

the very walls of our chamber accuse us, and repeat a long catalogue of our sins: and how terrible is it to think, that even what declares us to be righteous, in reality condemns us! for all that praises us, praises us only because it knows not the true balance in which we ought to be weighed.

What think ye now, my brethren? Do ye believe that in spite of the crimes they have committed, the Eternal Judge will spare sinners, and permit his avenging sword to rest in its scabbard? If he did so, he himself might be accused: he would then stand before the tribunal of his creatures, and sinners might appear against him, instead of his appearing against sinners. Justice and judgment would no longer be the foundation of his throne, and it would then be proved that his law and his denunciations had not been pronounced in earnest.

But this can never be so; the Bible tells us not only that *all* flesh has sinned, but that "judgment came upon *all* men to condemnation." The sentence of God has been passed upon all transgressors, and they are all doomed by an inexorable Judge to undergo a terrible death. In Paradise, it was pronounced over our fallen first parents. At the Flood, thousands in a fearful manner experienced its execution. On Sinai, it was once more formally proclaimed, "Cursed be he that continueth not in all the words of the law to do them!" On Ebal, this terrible denunciation displayed all its terrors. In the temple, we behold its symbol in the slaughter of the beasts for sacrifice. The prophets made the whole earth quake with its thunders. Christ, who had lain from all eternity in the bosom of the Father, confirmed it with his lips that cannot lie, and spake of the worm that never dies, and of the fire that is never quenched. Judas experienced the execution of this fearful sentence, for it had been better for him had he never been born. The spectacle of the rich man in flames and torment may help us to imagine its terrors ; and all the apostles join their voices together in telling us, that by nature we are children of wrath, and deserving of eternal death.

What then are we ? Prisoners on whom the sentence of death has been passed, and who can only expect a terrible end. We are lost creatures, to whom eternal pain and misery has been adjudged, in fire, with the devil and his angels. We carry our sentence about with us wherever we go, inscribed in an imperishable record, our names within, and God's seal confirming all. An appeal to another tribunal is absolutely impossible ; and equally so is escape from our imprisonment, for God's all-piercing eye searcheth everywhere. A supplication to our judge to remit his sentence, would also be in vain, for it would be desiring nothing less than that he would sacrifice justice and truth to caprice, and divest himself of his purity and holiness.

The decree has been pronounced ; the sentence is fixed, and must be put into execution. O that ye all might deeply experience the awfulness of this truth ! Many, however, are not aware that they carry about with them the document of their condemnation ; and with light hearts, those unfortunate ones go amusing themselves through the world. Some have a faint misgiving of the truth; but they strive to drown it in the bustle and tumult of life. Others try to blot out the characters in which their terrible sentence is written, by means of alms and God-service: but alas! they are ineffaceable! A few, and but a few, feel the burden of it weighing down their souls, and cry in piteous accents, "We are lost! we are lost!" Would to God there were more of the latter class among us! for it is to them we are commissioned to bear a most blessed and glorious message from the tribunal of Pilate.

Yes, for them the sentence of heavenly justice is remitted: it has disappeared, and is destroyed and annihilated, but not by caprice or partial favour. On the contrary, it has been put into execution, and not one of its terrors omitted; and yet,—can you comprehend it?—it has been lawfully annulled, and for ever done away with. Hearken to the terrible cry which resounds from before the tribunal of Pilate, "Crucify him! crucify him!" Listen to the awful words, "He is worthy of death! Away with him! Away with him! Let the blasphemer die!" Fearful and awful do they sound, enough to make us tremble! And at the same time, to the ear of faith, they are like the musical tones of the harp and lute! In these mystic words is comprehended the condemnation uttered in paradise, proclaimed on Mount Sinai, denounced from Ebal, promulgated by the prophets amongst the people, confirmed by Jesus Christ, and preached by the apostles to the whole world. This sentence of condemnation was pronounced over the pure head of our great Pledge; and the curse which had been uttered against us, now descended upon him. He was punished for our sins, and suffered for our misdeeds; for God did not even spare his only beloved Son, but sent him "in the likeness of sinful flesh, and for sin condemned sin in the flesh." Therefore it is written, "Christ hath redeemed us from the curse of the law, being made a curse for us." Therefore our Redeemer said to Pilate, "Thou couldest have no power at all against me, except it were given thee from above." Therefore the high priest prophesying, said, "It is expedient for us that one man should die for the people, and that the whole nation perish not." Therefore it is written, "And as it is appointed unto men once to die, but after this the judgment; so Christ was once offered to bear the sins of many." Therefore, we may say with Paul, "Who shall lay any thing to the charge of God's elect? It is God that justifieth. Who is he that condemneth? It is Christ that died."

II. The day on which the Son of God was condemned to death, was a day of justice and of divine vengeance upon sin, but at the same time a day to console the afflicted. Our history not only describes Jesus as the representative of sinners; but in the most vivid manner depicts the glorious and blessed consequences of his sufferings. Let us now read the twenty-fifth verse. "And he (Pilate) released unto them him that for sedition and murder was cast into prison, whom they had desired; but he delivered Jesus to their will." Most remarkable scene—surpassing every thing in mighty and important consequences !

Before I explain the wonderful allegory contained in our text, I shall recal to your minds a mysterious sacrificial ceremony described in the Old Testament. You are aware that yearly on the solemn feast-day, two goats were brought by the people to the high-priest ; after he had made atonement for himself and his household, by the sacrifice of a bull, he took the two first-mentioned animals, and cast lots upon them in the presence of the Lord. The one on which the lot fell, which was inscribed with the name of "Jehovah," was offered to God ; the other, that received the lot on which "Azazel" was written, was to go free. Thus the first was appointed to be a sin-offering unto the Lord ; and being regarded as laden with the sin and impurity of the second goat, which represented the people, was led to the slaughter—slain—and then carried outside the camp, where it was burned with fire, and its ashes scattered to the winds. When this was done, the goat Azazel, after the high-priest had confessed their misdeeds in the name of the people, was set at liberty, to wander through the fields and woods of the Holy Land, as during the journey from Egypt it had been released in the desert. Now it could pasture where it pleased, and run and enjoy itself wherever it would, for all in the land was at its option. No huntsman might shoot it, no husbandman prevent it feeding on his grounds ; for since the first goat had been slain for it, the Azazel was free as long as he lived ; none might imprison or injure it: and this was its right for ever.

It seems to me that the meaning of this holy ceremony is clear as day. It signified that One should come, who should take upon himself the sins of the people, be punished in their stead, and suffer death. Sinners would then be delivered from their curse, on account of the satisfaction made for them to Divine Justice; they would be like the Azazel, free and atoned for, and no longer under a sentence of condemnation.

This ceremony coincides in a most remarkable manner with the occurrence described in to-day's history; for it finds in it a literal fulfilment, in accordance undoubtedly with the eternal plan and counsel of God. Jesus and Barabbas stand together:—Barabbas, a rebel and a murderer; Jesus, a holy one, accused of crimes which Barabbas has committed. The murderer is a child of the devil; Jesus is the son of the Eternal Father, but it is said of him that he has a devil, and he is treated accordingly. As the lot was cast over the two goats in the temple, so, in like manner, the fate of the two prisoners is to be determined by a species of lot,—for, according to custom at the Passover, the people had it in their power to choose which of them should be set at liberty. Pilate now asked them, "Whom will ye that I release unto you? Barabbas, or Jesus, which is called Christ?" One of them must be set at liberty, and when once it is determined on, the choice remains unalterably fixed. As surely as one is set free, the other must suffer death; and one only can be saved, for the people have no right to demand more: at the same time, both cannot be put to death, for, according to law, one must go free. If Jesus be chosen, then woe to the murderer! If, on the contrary, the people demand Barabbas, then, alas for Jesus! he is lost, and the murderer escapes his rightful doom. Mysterious state of things! How then will the case be decided? You know already how the lot fell,—the happy lot, the lot of Azazel fell on Barabbas; for the people, as if with one voice, demanded the murderer to be set at liberty! The dark and bloody lot—the lot on which "Jehovah" was inscribed—fell on the blessed Jesus, and the Holy One must therefore be sacrificed. A most wonderful exchange now takes place, such as the world never saw;—the just one finds himself in the circumstances of the criminal, and the criminal is placed in the condition which rightfully belongs to the just. The innocent one suffers, as though on him lay the weight of the murderer's guilt; and the murderer is treated as though he were spotless and unstained. The chains of the evil-doer are laid upon the blameless; and liberty is announced to the evil-doer, as if to him belonged the rights of the blameless. The criminal's sentence of death is pronounced over the head of him who is more than angel pure, and the child of wrath thereby receives the right of quitting his prison and going whithersoever he pleases. In short, it is a full and perfect exchange of destiny: the scourges prepared for the rebel lacerate the back of the Son of God. On the cross erected for that child of the devil, there stands the inscription, "Jesus of

Nazareth ; and the transgressor rejoices in all the rights of the Prince of Peace, and receives the reward which should belong to the holy and just. Thus you behold the striking picture of all that used formerly to take place on the great Day of Atonement: the Lord Jesus is the sacrifice, the lot "Jehovah" destined to the sword ; while Barabbas is the "Azazel" free, and at liberty.

It is self-evident, my brethren, that the scene between Barabbas and Christ is also a symbol and parable. The murderer is our representative ; and in the same relation in which he stood to Jesus, we stand also to the Son of God. As this rebel could in no way have escaped the execution of his sentence, had he not been placed in mysterious connexion with Jesus, so, in like manner, neither could we. The death of the criminal appeared certain, until the question was asked, "Barabbas or Christ?" and then it was that the issue of the process seemed no longer doubtful. Had it been "Barabbas or any other person?" the detestable Barabbas never could have been chosen : the other would have been named, and then his death would have been certain. But as it was "Barabbas or the Nazarene?" the lot of freedom fell on Barabbas.

Thus, my brethren, had any other person, whether man or angel, placed himself in our situation to suffer for us, it would have done no good, for the sentence of death would still have rested upon us. Christ, however, placed himself in our stead—the Man that was not only holy, but who was God in the highest, and who in his own person did not require to suffer, nor yet to offer obedience: then that which had formerly seemed certain, I mean our condemnation, suddenly appeared doubtful: and I, who formerly must have exclaimed, "I am lost without hope!" could now say, "I or Christ Jesus!" Our deliverance was inseparably connected with his condemnation; and it was only by the lot of death falling upon him that our lives could be saved. Thus you perceive how we have as much to do as Barabbas with the scene before the judgment-seat of Pilate; and if from Barabbas a cry of joy broke forth when he heard the thousand voices exclaiming, "Crucify Jesus!" certainly our hearts should rejoice no less when we read the words, "And Pilate gave sentence that it should be as they required."

What a great and mysterious moment! Our cause was now eternally decided: the sentence of death was pronounced upon him; and he drew the lot that he was to atone for our sins, and suffer that curse with which we had been threatened. He has done it—Hallelujah! Since then we have been free; the sentence of death weighs us down no longer; our sins have lost their condemning power; and in our reckoning with God it is our merits through Christ, and not our debts, which preponderate. Henceforth death has lost its sting, and on our standard is inscribed the divine sentence—"Therefore as by the offence of one, judgment came upon all men to condemnation; even so by the righteousness of One, the free gift came upon all men unto justification of life."

III. Let us now contemplate this great matter; it

should not be thought of in church and on solemn days only, but it should be made matter of consideration daily, and in domestic life. It is a truth which should be grasped by the whole soul, and constantly made use of; not locked up like a medal in a cabinet, to be only viewed occasionally. It is a practical consolation which our hearts must receive and enjoy; it was for this purpose God gave it, Christ won it, and the Bible presents it to us on every side.

But you must be poor sinners before you can be refreshed by this consolation; since it is only for them that this honey drops out of the rock. You must feel your utter sinfulness, for a partial confession will not do; and the general terms, "I know I am imperfect and deficient in many things," is not sufficient. God would not have given up your Representative to an accursed death, and to the power of Satan for a time, had he not deemed you worthy of hell. Acknowledge, therefore, that the Eternal is just in the sentence he pronounces over you: say, "Yes, we are sinners!" and say it from the depth of your heart, and the bottom of your soul, in genuine humility. Nevertheless, you have no need to say it in despair, nor with anguish and wringing of hands; but say it with sorrow—a sorrow which cannot be cured until you experience that there exists One, who has taken upon himself the whole weight of the anger of God, which had otherwise rested upon you. Then, and then only, will Christ's passion be able to minister consolation to your hearts.

You must now regard Barabbas: as yet he knows

not that matters so important to him have taken place; and far from having any idea of the fortunate lot which has been cast for him, he sits in sullen despair on the floor of his dungeon, awaiting every moment the appearance of the officer who is to lead him to execution, —when, lo! there rushes in a breathless messenger, with joy depicted on his countenance, bringing the most incredible intelligence. "Hail to thee, Barabbas!" he cries out, "thou art free, thou art free!" and, even while he speaks, he is unchaining the astonished prisoner, and calling to him to arise and leave his confinement. In the first moment of astonishment, it seems to the criminal as though he were still dreaming; he then begins to think that he has been permitted, for a few hours, to walk about the court of his prison, to which he must return after enjoying for a short space the free air of heaven. The messenger, however, assures him anew that he is free, and explain how the thing has taken place. Thus Barabbas learns that the sentence of death no longer impends over his head, for it has been annulled and torn; that he has nothing more to do with offended justice, for he has been restored to the rights of a citizen, and no complaints will henceforth be raised against him; on the contrary, he will be treated as though he never had committed a crime; and all this has been done, because another has stood in his place, and suffered death on the cross instead of him. The messenger who brings him this blessed intelligence, withholds nothing, but declares it freely and fully; and is he not in this the type of a faithful evangelist? Yes, ye souls that are weary and heavy-laden, a message similar to what the murderer received is now conveyed to you, only far greater and far more blessed. In clear and simple terms we declare, that since the great exchange took place, before the judgment-seat of Pilate and on Mount Golgotha, there is no more condemnation for you that are in Christ Jesus. And we entreat you to receive this word in faith and humility, for we speak it in Christ's stead, and we bring you the message in the name of God.

The manner in which Barabbas received the joyful intelligence of his being set free, has not been disclosed to us; nevertheless, let us contemplate the subject for a few moments. If Barabbas, filled with a sense of the magnitude of his crime, had regarded the message as jest and mockery, and instead of availing himself of his offered freedom, had resisted the removal of his chains, and expressed his determination to remain in imprisonment, would ye not have called him a fool? Ye would, my brethren; but in doing so, ye would condemn yourselves; for do not the greater part of Christians act in the same manner? Suppose, on the other hand, he had contradicted the intelligence communicated to him by the herald, saying, "It is impossible that your message can be true:" would it not have been virtually accusing, in the severest terms, the government, in whose name the officer came, by giving all of them the lie? Think upon this, ye weak and timid Christians, who will neither believe Christ nor his apostles, when they tell you that there is "no condemnation to them which are in Christ Jesus!" Suppose, again, that Barabbas, on receiving the announcement of his freedom, had replied, "No, I dare not leave my prison; I will first become a new man, and when I have proved my amendment, then set me free!" What would the messenger have replied? "If thou supposest," he might say, "that thou art to be set at liberty for thine own sake, then know that it can never be the case; for the crime which thou didst commit, cannot be undone even by thy amendment. In the sight of the law, thou wilt always be a murderer, and worthy of death; therefore make use of this free and undeserved mercy, for according to strict justice thou canst be set free!" Weigh well in your hearts, my brethren, these supposed words, for they have deep signification.

To take another view of the question: Barabbas might have said, "No! I shall remain a prisoner, until I become as useful a member of society, as I was formerly a pest to my fellow-creatures!" Think you this would have sounded nobly? Would it not rather have been a new piece of folly? "Foolish man!" they might have answered him, "before you can be useful to society, you must be at liberty; for how can you attain your object, bound in chains, and lying in a dungeon?" You must attentively consider this reply also: for are there not many amongst us who wish to become holy before being justified and made free in Christ Jesus? Alas! they will find it impossible!

None of those thoughts, in all probability, entered the mind of Barabbas; he would, on the contrary, give himself up to joy, on receiving the joyful intelligence

—throw aside his chains—quit his darksome dungeon—exchange the garb of a delinquent for one more honourable,—and instantly make use of his offered freedom. Transported with delight, he would return to the bosom of his family, and free and unshackled, move about whithersoever he pleased. He would not be afraid to appear even in the presence of his judges; for who could accuse him, who, instead of making his escape from prison, had been judicially set free? And even although some are sceptical, and refuse to believe that he has been lawfully released, can he not assure them that Jesus of Nazareth has suffered crucifixion in his stead, and will not the thing then become intelligible? Even though he dream for a moment that he is still sitting in his dungeon, he has only to feel his hands and feet, to see if the chains are still encompassing him: happily for him they are removed, and on perceiving this, he experiences the blessed conviction that he is at liberty. In this also, as in every thing else, you must follow the example of Barabbas; and if your deliverance from the power of sin appear doubtful, you must examine if you are still bound by its chains, or if you are loosed from its bonds, and no longer under its dominion. If, on the contrary, you are filled with detestation towards it, and armed against its approaches, you have a sure proof that the freedom of the children of God has begun in you also.

The doubt, perhaps, arises in your heart, that the satisfaction made by your Redeemer has not been sufficient for you, on account of the appalling amount of sin and iniquity you have committed. If so, my brethren, look to the last scene of your Mediator's life, and contemplate the dying thief on the cross! What a spectacle of mercy! a sinner borne by angels into paradise! God receives him in his arms, calls him his own and well-beloved child, sets a crown of glory upon his head, and, as though he beheld nothing in him but perfection and beauty, assures him of paradise for his inheritance! Is not this great and astonishing? Measure then by this man the fruit of the sacrifice of Christ; for surely his blood must be of wonderful efficacy to produce such glorious results to poor and miserable sinners!

And now, one more consideration. You have heard that according to the command of God, the goat Azazel was to be set free, and no more exposed to peril or danger; he was to be allowed to go wherever he pleased, and no one might confine or injure him. But are you aware of what took place in after-times, when the spiritual deterioration of Israel began, and the word of God was no longer regarded? They understood so little the proper sense of the sacrificial ceremony on the great day of atonement, that they were accustomed, after setting the goat Azazel free, to hunt it through the meadows and fields, and when they had caught it, to throw it down from a rock, and break its neck. Blindness unparalleled! Truly, in doing so, the Jews only spoke their own condemnation, and proved that they had no desire to participate in redemption. And now, ye Azazels, ye who have become free through Christ's blood, it might so happen that ye were treated in a similar manner; that people might pursue you, deny your freedom in Christ Jesus, and crying out, "Do this and that first!" strive to rob you of your consciousness of safety, and thus spiritually treat you like the Azazels of later times. Say, when this happens, "These people are Jews, who do not understand the true signification and importance of the mighty sacrifice which has been offered for them!" And never forget that God has ordained that the Azazel should be free and unharmed; and that no man should lay hands upon him!

THE EASTER MESSAGE

MARK XVI. 1—7

And when the Sabbath was past, Mary Magadalene, and Mary the mother of James, and Salome, had bought sweet spices, that they might come and anoint him. And very early in the morning, the first day of the week, they came into the sepulchre at the rising of the sun. And they said among themselves, Who shall roll us away the stone from the door of the sepulchre? And when they looked, they saw that the stone was rolled away: for it was very great. And entering into the sepulchre, they saw a young man sitting on the right side, clothed in a long white garment: and they were affrighted. And he saith unto them, Be not affrighted: ye seek Jesus of Nazareth, which was crucified: he is risen; he is not here behold the place where they laid him. But go your way, tell his disciples and Peter that he goeth before you into Galilee there shall ye see him, as he said unto you.

THIS, my brethren, is the Gospel for this joyful feast-day. Like a tower it stands pre-eminent; and every word in it is like a bell chiming gladly, the harbinger of peace. From it there springs up a fountain of joy which far surpasses human understanding; and a rock of truth rises in the midst, on which we may repose our wearied wings, and rest from the tumult and turmoil of life. The first part of our history presents us with a mournful picture: but this is done intentionally, to make the splendour of Easter consolation shine more brightly from a dark back-ground. We are transported amongst the mourning women, who, with weeping eyes, left their cottages before the break of day, and hastened, with sweet spices, to the grave of their beloved Master; forgetful at first, in their all-absorbing grief, that they had no one to roll away the stone from the door of the sepulchre. When they now, with anxious looks, turn towards each other, and in perplexity inquire who should roll it away for them, can we imagine a more melancholy scene? And does it not show us how dark and dismal our life would be, were it not enlivened by the Easter sun? I also stood, like those women, a sorrowing orphan in this vale of tears; and who was there to say to me, "Weep not!" for stone above stone I saw lying before me, of whose removal I might well despair. My sin, like a gigantic rock, almost obscured the heaven above me; and who was there to say, "Be comforted!" when I lamented that my transgressions were more than could be forgiven? The women, however, advanced nearer the tomb, and I along with them. What do I see? Hallelujah! The stone is rolled away, and with it all that oppressed me. The grave is open—the sun has arisen, and angels clad in white welcome us with a smile; while one of them cries out, in accents which thrill our very souls, "Ye seek Jesus of Nazareth, which was crucified: he is risen; he is not here; behold the place where they laid him!"

This is indeed a message of joy, or I know no what merits that appellation. Let us pause at these words of the angel, and contemplate, in the miracle of the resurrection, the glory of the Eternal Father, the glory of the Son, and the glory of his chosen ones.

I. The text, "The Lord is risen!" seems to us a song of praise addressed to him that sitteth upon the throne; it dispels the clouds that hang over our heads, and, like a flaming torch ascending upwards into heaven, shows us, by its light, the glory of Him to whom Jesus alluded when he said, "He is near that justifieth me: who will contend with me?" and of whom it is written, "Righteousness and judgment are the habitation of his throne!" We realized the presence of this great Being during the earthquake on Golgotha—and trembled. We beheld him under a new aspect at the Resurrection—and rejoiced: for the Son had now finished the work which his Father had enjoined him. He had re-established that law which had been put to shame, and had offered an obedience such as could satisfy even the demands of God. He has risen victorious over the attacks of hell; the fiery darts of every conceivable temptation have been turned aside on the buckler of his faith; he has preserved unshaken his confidence in God, in situations where the highest seraph might have despaired; and proved himself subject to the will of his Father in all things, by undergoing an ignominious and accursed death. For all this he is now worthy, fully worthy, of the rich and glorious reward appointed for him by the eternal counsel of his Father: it belongs to him by the justest of all claims: and his work being now accomplished, the Son of Mary merits to be crowned with glory, according to the holy promises of God. Lo! this crowning takes place before our very eyes! Scarcely has the morning-star announced the dawn of the third day, when the eternal covenant of truth shines in all its splendour from the heavens: the Almighty keeps his word; and his hands are laden with garlands for the Victor. The Hero is still sleeping silently and calmly in his chamber, and hell is still rejoicing in the idea that it has obtained the mastery, when suddenly the voice of the Almighty penetrates the tomb: the word, "Arise!" is pronounced over the bloody corpse;—in an instant the bandages are loosened, and the linen cloth is removed which enveloped the countenance; the stream of immortal life gushes through the hitherto stiffened limbs; the form of a servant has disappeared, and the Son of Man rises from the dust in unspeakable glory and brightness. Even heaven is set in motion, and the angels of God descend to pay homage to the Prince of Life. A seraph opens for his Lord the door of the tomb, and the earth trembles with joy under the feet of its glorified King; the stones call out "Hosanna," and the rocks rending asunder are his hymns of praise; the guards who watched his tomb, the representatives of his enemies, now overpowered by his majesty, lie, like dead men, on the ground at his feet; the saints, after the slumber of thousands of years, rise out of their graves to bear witness that the land of death has been conquered, and the power of death taken away. Nature, adorned in the fairest colours of spring, seems in silent adoration to solemnize the triumph of her Creator; and the sun, which is even now issuing forth in all its glory from the flaming gates of the firmament, appears to be ascending for no other purpose than to swell the coronation splendour of the great Prince of Life!

Amidst these glorious signs and wonders, Jehovah summons our great Pledge out of his prison-house. What a moment of delight this is to the heart of the Eternal Father, when, after all the condemnation which had been passed on Him that was despised and rejected of men, he now opposes his sentence to the sentence of the enemies of his Son—both those that are human and the powers of hell. The miracle of the resurrection seems to me like the voice of the Eternal God, proclaiming through heaven, earth, and hell, "This is my beloved Son, in whom I am well pleased!" and is a solemn vindication of him whom the world esteemed worthy of death. It is the mighty protest of Jehovah against all the accusations heaped by the Israelites upon our holy Redeemer, and is a divine declaration louder than thunder, "that the All-Righteous One has accomplished his work, and paid our debts to the uttermost farthing!" The resurrection was as if Heaven had set its seal on the deed of our acquittal; and the stone which the builders rejected thus became the head-stone of the corner. It was Jehovah's recommendation of his Son to the whole world; and proclaimed louder than words could have uttered, This is the Redeemer of men! happy are they that trust in him!

II. Now that we have contemplated the Father, the God of truth and righteousness, in the Easter miracle, let us direct our attention to the Easter King himself, who rises before us encompassed with such a heaven of beauty, majesty, and splendour, that it seems incomprehensible that there should be one in the whole world who could refrain from bowing the knee on beholding him. No, we have never seen Jesus as he now appears bursting from the tomb! We saw him when he said unto the devils, "Come out of him!" and they came: we saw him when he rebuked the raging elements; and we broke forth into the cry of astonishment, "What manner of man is this, that even the winds and the waves obey him!" We saw him when, monarch of nature, he trod upon the billows, which became like rocks under his feet; and when he called into the abode of corruption, "Lazarus, come forth!" and the dead man arose, and left his prison-house. But all this glory and splendour falls far short of that in which he rises to-day, phœnix-like, from his own ashes. Amidst all his previous wonders and miracles, he was not so highly exalted as now, at the moment when we greet him with our hallelujahs in the garden of Joseph. If we imagine him as we last beheld him, suffering the pains of martyrdom, and the weight of our sins oppressing him,—when, forsaken by God and by every creature, he was nailed to the cross, and being made a curse for us, was rejected both by heaven and earth,—we can scarcely believe that we behold the same Jesus in the glorious form rising from the sepulchre. Yet he is the same, the same as he who once bore the curse of our sins; and it is this which makes us wonder and rejoice to-day. Lo! he stands above his tomb, a victorious hero, overpowered by death indeed, but only for a time; for death is now dead in him, and has for ever yielded to his supremacy. The melancholy picture which we beheld on Mount Golgotha can no longer be discerned: the body of weakness, the tabernacle of feeble flesh,—the heavy and earthly covering, a prey to the fury of the elements,—the mortal form, in which he atoned for our sins, all has been left behind him in the tomb. In Christ, who formerly was despised and rejected of men, a man of sorrows and acquainted with grief, we now behold a glorified being that can no longer suffer or die any more; for his body has received immortal life, and the splendour of unchangeable brightness; and in his soul there is a paradise of peace and a heaven of joy and delight. There is no longer a trace in his heart of sorrow and suffering, struggle and trial: his wounds are for ever closed, and his soul only experiences the approbation of his Father, the enjoyment of the love of God, and the constant sensation of his presence. Hell lies conquered under his feet, for it beholds the thunderbolt in his hand which could in an instant annihilate it. The accusers are ashamed and silent, and no longer open their mouths; for they see that even the snow of angel-purity would appear dark when viewed in the light which emanates from the breastplate of our great High Priest. The angels surround him, and rest under the shadow of his wings; for they feel that life is in his breath, and peace in his presence. Thus the Prince of Easter stands clad in a glory which fills both heaven and earth; the King of Earth, which he hath bought with his blood, and King of Heaven, which now greets him with rejoicing, because the Son of Man is about to mount the throne of eternal majesty.

III. But of what avail is it to us that Christ is so beautiful and glorious? and how are we benefited by it? Well may you ask the question, for it is of the utmost importance to us all. If we belong to Christ, that is to say, if we rest upon him in faith with the ardour of our whole hearts, then are we partakers in the beauty, splendour, and victorious glory in which he rises from the tomb, for he is ours in all his majesty and greatness: and this is our great joy in contemplating the Easter miracle. Perhaps ye think that I am speaking figuratively—not so, I speak literally; or that I allude to a glory of which we shall be partakers hereafter—but there also ye are mistaken, for we are partakers of it already. While I declare to you those astonishing things, I have not sand, but rocks under my feet; and my intelligence is not airy and unsubstantial, but dug out of the great mine of the word of God; for have you not observed that the hearts and mouths of the apostles are full of this thing, and that this is the great spring of their unutterable joy, their unspeakable delight, and their lofty courage, with which they contemned difficulty and death? Consider the subject for a moment, and you will find it so; for how otherwise could they have been happy in this evil world, smiling at the impotency of death, hell, and the devil, had they not rested securely on the great article of the resurrection of Christ?

We must now contemplate the subject more nearly.

The great importance of the resurrection of Christ, and the great subject for consolation which it affords, are generally found in two circumstances; that thereby the validity of the sacrifice on the cross was divinely proclaimed, and that a seal and pledge was given to us of our own future resurrection. These are precious and undoubted truths; but there is a third circumstance, frequently overlooked, which ought to be taken into consideration before all others, for it is the point in the Easter miracle from which beams the greatest light and splendour.

You know the words of Paul, in Romans iv. 25: when speaking of Christ, he says, "who was delivered for our offences, and was raised again for our justification." From this text you may discern the heart-enrapturing truth which I am about to announce to you. For our sins he was forsaken by God; and the whole sum of our transgressions, which should stand recorded against us in the great book at the last day, was in a mysterious manner attributed to him. He made atonement for them, and bare the curse, which otherwise would have fallen upon us and caused our eternal damnation. I am free and at liberty; but this negative principle does not include the whole efficacy of the mediatorship and atonement of Christ: my situation is not that of a criminal whom the mercy of his king has permitted to escape his merited punishment; but through Jesus I have entered into the rights of a child, I have become sanctified through him, an object of love to my heavenly Father, and an heir of eternal life. All this was declared to me by the miracle-of the third day, and on the wings of Easter morning this mighty and incomparable consolation flew to greet me.

It was of his own free-will that Jesus tasted of death; love prompted him, otherwise he needed not to have done so. Death was not due to him, for in his own person eternal life belonged to him; but he was willing to suffer our doom, and it is therefore we behold in him the unheard-of spectacle of a man all pure and holy treated by God as a sinner. To the glory, also, in which we behold him clad on the third day, he stands in quite another relation than he did to his sufferings; for the latter did not personally belong to him, but the former was his due: he had a right to it, and was worthy of it, for he had won and deserved it by his obedience. But for whom had he won it? For himself? Of what use could it have been to him, to whom all belonged already, as being one with the Father? You must now call to mind that in all his actions and sufferings he stood in our place, and fulfilled in our name the work of his Father; thus earning for us its fruit and reward, and receiving for us, after his resurrection, the garland and the crown from the hands of his eternal Judge and Rewarder.

There is an expression of our Redeemer in the Gospel of St. John x. 17, which particularly merits our attention: "Therefore doth my Father love me, because I lay down my life, that I might take it again." This verse appears at first sight mysterious, and that in more than one respect. The first thing which astonishes us, is the cause to which Jesus attributes the love of his Father: we had hitherto imagined that Jesus was beloved by God because he was his Son, "the brightness of his glory, and the express image of his person;" but here Jesus assures us that the cause of his Father's love towards him is his laying down his life for sinners. Jesus does not speak of himself here as the Word, which was from the beginning with God, and which was God; but as of another person, who, by the execution of certain conditions, merits the Father's love and approbation. It is obvious that Jesus, in this expression, does not allude to the love with which Jehovah loved him through all eternity; but to another love, which he, the Mediator, and the Second Adam, should win for his sinful people as their pledge and representative. And this love of God, in which men become partakers through Jesus Christ, could not have been attained but by his death, which has made atonement for our sins, and satisfied divine justice in our stead. Henceforward, therefore, God does not love Jesus as his only-begotten Son merely; he loves him also as our Head, and in him he loves sinners. This explains the first mystery; but there is a still deeper and holier signification in the words, "Therefore doth my Father love me, because I lay down my life." But why does he lay down his life? "That I might take it again!" is the answer; and it is not temporal life alone of which Jesus here speaks. The word "life" comprehends all that glory which the Son enjoyed with the Father from the beginning, and of which he now divested himself. Willingly he gave up this divine glory and happiness, and received in their place the punishment of an accursed transgressor; doing this, as we hear, for no other purpose than to resume them afterwards. Here is another mystery, for is it not strange that Jesus should quit an existence of blessedness for no other reason than to enter upon it again after a short and bloody intermission? At first sight nothing could appear more extraordinary; but who will venture to attribute an action without an object to the Lord of heaven? No, it was to save us that our Redeemer resolved upon divesting himself of his life and glory: he gave them away, in order to reassume them after enduring the cross, but in a different manner from that in which they belonged to him before; formerly they had been for himself alone, now he gave them to his people also. He left his glory for a time, in order to obtain the right of imparting it to others, and of making the righteousness of the Son of God the general property of those that believe in his name.

The glory which we behold Jesus receiving as he ascends from the tomb is certainly that which he has long possessed, but at the same time is that which now belongs to us; for he does not now possess it in consequence of his birth and existence in the Father, but as our pledge and representative. And this, my brethren, is the great fountain of consolation and peace presented to us by the Easter miracle. When I hear the announcement, "Christ is risen!" not only do I think of Christ, but it seems to me as though I also were risen. When I view him as the Holy and Righteous One, triumphing over sin, the world, and hell,—as the

Conqueror who has slain death, bound and vanquished Satan, won himself a throne in the heavens, and now enjoys the divine love and approbation,—I need not then say, "How glorious *thou* art!" On the contrary, I must appropriate to myself all his glory, crown myself with his victorious garland, make his consciousness of innocence my own; and all that I see in him great and desirable, I must regard as a treasure which I am not merely to receive in future, but which through him I already possess, though it may be only as a foretaste. "The words, 'Christ is risen from the dead,'" says Luther, "should be inscribed in such large letters that we should be unable to see any thing else, not even heaven and earth. Christ's resurrection and victory over sin, death, and hell, however great we may imagine them, are still greater; and a thousand hells, and a hundred thousand deaths, would be but as a spark and a drop compared to his resurrection, victory, and triumph. Christ, however, has given away his resurrection, victory, and triumph, to all who believe on him. If we, therefore, believe upon him, it follows, that though sin, death, and hell, were leagued against us, we should have no cause of alarm, for they could not hurt us. In Christ we are holy by means of faith, although we are still sinners; and we know that however deficient we may be, yet Jesus our Lord and Head has risen from the dead; he has no sin, and there is no more death in him; and so in him we have no longer either sin or death. God has called Jesus from the grave, restored him to life, and raised him up to heaven, in order that he may henceforward reign over all. Where now is sin? He has trampled it under foot: and I need no longer be timid and fearful, for through Christ I have a clear conscience, and am without sin. I may now bid defiance to death and the devil, sin and hell, for they can do me no injury, Death! where is thy sting? Sin, where is thy power? Christ has taken away sin from those that believe, so that they are now spotless, like himself, and through him have overcome death, the devil, and hell. If we believe, then may we say that we have both lived and died; for faith teaches us that Christ did not rise from the dead in his own person merely, but that we also rose along with him, and along with him shall enjoy eternal life. Paul says, in Ephesians ii. 6. that God 'hath raised us up together, and made us sit together in heavenly places in Christ Jesus.' This, however, is still concealed, and not yet made manifest. Nevertheless, ye must regard this doctrine, and keep it so constantly in your view, as to see nothing else in heaven and earth. Even though a Christian die, and the dead corpse is buried, and the picture and the sounds of death greet both your eyes and ears; yet through faith ye must behold and hear things very different, ye must be as though ye did not perceive the grave and the corpse, but as if ye perceived life in the midst of a blooming garden, or a green meadow filled with living and happy beings."

These are Luther's words, and this was the opinion of the great reformer of our church with regard to the resurrection, in which he coincides exactly with that of all the holy apostles. In contemplating the Easter miracle, they never for a moment lost sight of the important doctrine of Christ being our representative. Their first and most earnest inquiry always was, What made the Lord Jesus be so peculiarly exalted and glorified on the third day by his heavenly Father? Then were they told that Jesus our great Pledge did not receive this honour as the Word which had been with the Father from the beginning; but as the representative of man, in whose name he had fulfilled those conditions with which God had indissolubly connected the promise of his grace and of eternal life; and that in the most wonderful manner he had ceased for a time (if I may so speak) to be the Apostle and immaculate Son of God, and had, on the contrary, become a sinner in the eyes of his Father. For this reason, they were told, he received from Jehovah, in the garden of Joseph, the actual and visible testimony, that nothing more could be required from him; and this was done by his glorious resurrection, in which he was declared worthy of a throne in the heavens: this declaration not concerning him alone, but those sinners also in whose place he stood. Spiritually speaking, their heads were there also, while garlands and crowns were showered down upon their Pledge; they might appropriate to themselves the glory of the resurrection, and believe that they heard the words of the Father pronounced over them, "This is my beloved son, in whom I am well pleased!" Therefore they may cry, rejoicing, (" God) hath quickened us together with Christ; and hath raised us up together, and made us sit together in heavenly places in Christ Jesus." Therefore they may consider themselves as already sitting in heaven, and as if they beheld sin and the grave, death and hell, lying under their feet; for they no longer know themselves except as in their glorified Pledge, and they regard all his treasures, his glory and his victory, as their own. Is it to be wondered at, that, being clad in such an armour of faith, they should regard their adversaries with indifference? No threatening on the part of the world can terrify them, no attack of the powers of evil alarm them; even the conviction of their own frailty and imperfection does not decrease their joyfulness; and the dark grave, instead of casting a shadow before them, sends forth the light of hope to cheer their daily pilgrimage. They have overcome all in the person of their Redeemer; and no longer as combatants, but as victors, they occupy the field.

Alas! my brethren, the blessed efficacy of the gospel is seen but little among us, and it is a sad, oppressed, and melancholy Christendom which surrounds us. We know too little the springs of strength and joy which lie around us, and with the most blessed portions of the New Testament we are shamefully unacquainted; hence the inefficiency of our measures, hence the despondency in the midst of us. We have a glory in Christ Jesus which surpasses all understanding; as yet it is not manifest; but what will it be when it is declared to us? Then, heaven and earth will be too narrow; all must become new, and all must be changed, to keep pace with the glory of the saints, and to be a suitable scene and habitation for the royal priesthood of the chosen ones. A hasty and transient glimpse, such as we have now, of our glory in Christ Jesus, cannot adequately transport and enliven our hearts; we ought to contemplate it constantly, beholding its splendour by means of faith, mounting like eagles towards the sun, and leaving the night of this earth far behind us. The stream on the banks of which the trees are always green, both summer and winter, has its source in the Easter miracle; and the tones of the harp which drives away all the spirits of evil, are still heard floating in the air above Joseph's garden.

The moment after Paul has exhorted Timothy to strive for the faith, and to arm himself for combat, he thus addresses him: "Remember that Jesus Christ, of the seed of David, was raised from the dead, according to my gospel!"—thus doing his utmost to impress a vivid picture on the soul of his friend, which might remain there daily and hourly, and be ever present to his view in unfading clearness and eternal brightness, to the exclusion of all other images. And whose picture was this? My brethren, ye have heard: it was the picture of Jesus Christ—not the crucified One, but the beautiful and glorious Lord risen from the dead; it was the triumphant portrait of the Conqueror of death.

Paul seems to have been of opinion that the sight of the glorious image of Christ enshrined in the temple of his heart, must be of the utmost service to Timothy while in this world's scene of struggle. He himself had experienced what heroic courage a glance at the Easter miracle could impart; and on reading his epistles, we cannot doubt that the spring of his boldness, his long-suffering, and his joy, might be found in the contemplation of Jesus on the third day. And in order that Timothy may experience the same thing, he calls out to him, " Remember that Jesus Christ, of the seed of David, was raised from the dead!"

Yes, my brethren, there is wafted from the picture of the resurrection, a balsamic fragrance, whose quickening and enlivening influence is not to be described. A light proceeds from it, by whose illumination all that formerly terrified us is seen lying under our feet, and even the dark termination of our existence, the terrific grave itself, is clad with a heavenly brightness. Can we then give you a more glorious exhortation than this, ' Remember that Jesus Christ was raised from the dead!" For true it is what Luther says, " The more a Christian contemplates the picture of the resurrection, the more he is blessed in Christ Jesus!" And O, may the Spirit paint this beautiful portrait with always brighter and brighter colours in our souls, and may he give us to understand its deep signification! May he enable us to comprehend how we sit on the same throne with our glorified Lord, and may he help us to decipher the mysterious handwriting of God in the Easter miracles, so that we may have boldness to exclaim with Paul from the depth of our souls, " Who is he that condemneth? It is Christ that died, yea, rather, that is risen again, who is even at the right hand of God, who also maketh intercession for us!" Amen.

THE EASTER MORNING

John xx. 11—17

But Mary stood without at the sepulchre weeping: and as she wept, she stooped down, and looked into the sepulchre, and seeth two angels in white sitting, the one at the head, and the other at the feet, where the body of Jesus had lain. And they say unto her, Woman, why weepest thou? She saith unto them, Because they have taken away my Lord, and I know not where they have laid him. And when she had thus said, she turned herself back, and saw Jesus standing, and knew not that it was Jesus. Jesus saith unto her, Woman, why weepest thou? whom seekest thou? She, supposing him to be the gardener, saith unto him, Sir, if thou have borne him hence, tell me where thou hast laid him, and I will take him away. Jesus saith unto her, Mary! She turned herself, and saith unto him, Rabboni; which is to say, Master! Jesus saith unto her, Touch me not; for I am not yet ascended to my Father: but go to my brethren, and say unto them, I ascend unto my Father, and your Father; and to my God, and your God.

This is perhaps the most beautiful and the most deeply interesting narrative in the whole Bible. It is like a picture representing a heavenly scene, the colours of which are formed by the bright and variegated dusts found in the cups of flowers. It is like a clear and full-toned chord struck on the Easter harp; or a mirror reflecting that glorified existence, whose loveliness our finest ideal creations sketch only imperfectly.

Yes, it belonged to the pen of the disciple who lay on the bosom of Jesus, to describe a scene unequalled in spiritual beauty and tenderness; upon which dawned the morning of that day which shall witness no more tears, unless it be tears of joy. How wonderful and how comforting is all that this picture represents, and how gladdening are the accents in which it addresses our spirits! It is indeed an Easter gospel, tidings of good news; and as such may it benefit our souls!

I. Wonderful! that the most glorious and the most joyful morning which ever dawned on this sinful world, should by the children of God be ushered in with tears! The brethren must first experience from the bottom of their souls how wretched their condition would have been if their Lord and Master had continued in the tomb; then would the joy which Easter brings strike deeper root in their hearts. There are certain truths, and certain sorrowful facts, which must be first acknowledged and experienced, before the blessed signification and importance of the resurrection be fully understood and appreciated. They are as follows: that we are by nature lost; that the curse of the law rests upon us; that it were but just had we been given over to the powers of evil; that all the intellect of man is unable to throw light on the gloomy mystery of the tomb; that if there were indeed a life beyond the grave, it could only be, to beings estranged from God as we are, a life of terror and woe. These bitter thoughts must sink deep into our hearts; for not until we have drunk of this cup of wormwood shall we be able to exclaim, "the joy of Easter is transcendent!"

and not until then shall we be able to understand the joy of Mary in the garden of Joseph.

It is indeed a glorious morning now dawning around us; its brilliancy is just beginning to gild the blue canopy of heaven; the fields are glittering with dewy pearls, and the trees are waving their branches in the morning wind. How silent and how sabbath-like every thing appears! all seems awaiting the celebration of some great festival; it is as though nature anticipated what was about to happen. The song of the birds sounds more joyously from the thickets; heaven looks down upon earth with a different aspect; even the flowers bloom more brightly than usual on the plains; and mountains, meadows, plants, and trees, seem to participate in one common gladness; every heart beats in silent delight and rapturous anticipation. Why then is this mournful women so sad? Alas! she anticipates nothing; and the most beautiful morning the world ever saw brings only grief to her, and weeping is the salutation with which she greets it. How ardently does she desire the songters among the bushes to be silent, and the morning to dawn more slowly! for a dark and cloudy heaven, a cold autumnal wind, and a sad dirge of death and the grave, would suit the feelings of her heart far better than the gay and lovely spring which is blooming around her. Behold her standing oppressed with sorrow, leaning against the rock, her face covered with her hands! She hardly knows where she is, or what she is doing; only one thing is she conscious of, that she is the most miserable being in the whole world, and the most deserving of pity; far more does she suffer than those who have lost their dearest friend, far more than even the blessed Virgin. Who then is this lonely one in Joseph's garden, whose eyes are red with weeping, and who could scarcely be more sad were she mourning the death of father and mother, and were she left a poor and friendless orphan in this cold and cheerless world? She is Mary Magdalene, she who has been named the Peter of the female disciples, and who we feared would have died from the excess of her grief and despair at beholding the sufferings of Him on whom her whole soul depended; but our dying Lord sustained her from his cross with invisible hands; and had it not been for this, the weary eyes of Mary had ceased to weep, for her heart had been broken.

No one felt more bitterly the truths which we alluded to at the beginning of our discourse, than Mary Magdalene. She knew, from sad experience, the condition of the lost sheep and of fallen man, for she had been sunk in the depths of misery and guilt. She had felt the power of sin, the anger and the curse of God, the terrors of hell, and the temptations of the powers of evil. She had been pre-eminent in wickedness; seven devils had had possession of her: the weight of her sins had reduced her to the brink of despair; and in her own person she had experienced the gnawing of the worm that never dies. Yet she had not been left alone in her misery, for at the moment when she would otherwise have sunk, she was sustained by the hand of love, and she found a Man who said to her in the name of God, "Thy sins are forgiven!" a

Man who in an instant released her from the fearful bondage under which she had groaned for years; who assured her that God loved her, sinner though she was; and who opened to her views of eternity which transported her heart with joy. Ever since that time, this Man had been the object that filled her soul; she had followed him whithersoever he went, and had never left him; for he was her all in this world. But, alas! what had she not suffered for this Beloved One? He had come to a fearful and terrible end;—as one forsaken both by God and man, he had died on the accursed tree; and no hand had been stretched from the clouds to save him, and no voice had been heard from above to exculpate him. From that hour Mary's heaven had been in ruins: and who can wonder! This Man had been the foundation of her peace, and the stronghold of her hope; for peace she had never known until the Sinner's Friend had assured her of it, and hope she never had until he had pledged himself for the truth of her expectations. If he were dead, then all would be dead to Mary—her peace, her joy, nay, every consolation both in time and eternity. And were he indeed to remain in the grave, then, alas! he could not be the Man from heaven; he had no right to absolve accursed sinners; and his actions could not be well pleasing to Jehovah. "If this be the case," thought Magdalene, "I am indeed miserable, for alas! he had no authority to say 'Her sins which are many are forgiven!' Then I am indeed accursed by God; then will hell with renewed rage overpower me, and my path will once more lead down to the abyss!"

Oppressed by thoughts such as these, Mary, wretched beyond measure, joined on the evening of Friday those who accompanied the beloved corpse to the tomb. Now for the last time she bathed it with her tears—but, alas! immeasurably more bitter tears than those with which she had washed his feet in the house of Simon. Yet even while she wept, her sorrow was cheered at intervals by the twilight of hope. The Jewish Sabbath meanwhile passed over, and the hours of the succeeding sleepless night were spent in grief and lamentation until the dawn of the third day, when she arose in haste, and was the first to be found in Joseph's garden. When it was yet dark, says our history, she who had hastened before the other disciples arrived at the sepulchre: but what did she behold? The stone rolled away, and the prison-house of death empty! A cold shiver ran through her limbs; but did a thought of the resurrection occur to her? Alas, no! Her first idea was, that his enemies had stolen away the dead body of her beloved Master: her thoughts were, "Now I have nothing more to do with man, and my hopes are for ever dashed to pieces!" This belief took such a firm hold of her mind, that even when the taper of hope began to glimmer, its feeble and trembling light was unable to penetrate the gloomy clouds which overshadowed her soul.

II. Bowed to the ground by thoughts such as these, Mary advanced to the sepulchre, and leaned against the rock. Was she not unutterably miserable—hurled suddenly, as she had been, out of a heaven of peace and joy, into a night whose darkness no star could penetrate? If things really were as she supposed, what a house of misery this world would be! and how would all of us mingle our tears together! Praised be God, however, things are different—quite, quite different! Yet we cannot look without emotion on the woman weeping by the tomb; though we know at the same time that her sorrow cannot touch her heart too deeply, since it is so soon to be changed into unutterable joy. Imagine her feelings, were she to hear a voice say to her, "Mary, dost thou observe nothing? Do no blissful anticipations thrill through thy soul? Look around thee! Observe the stone rolled aside; the rocks torn asunder; the wonderful order in the tomb, and the napkin wrapped together, apart from the linen clothes! Dost thou not behold that all nature is worshipping in silent adoration, that every created thing is holding some mighty festival, and even the sun is ascending the firmament more joyfully? Mary, however, hears none of this; and voices louder and deeper must be heard ere she can be awakened out of her gloomy reverie. She now bends down and looks into the grave: has she still no misgiving? Alas! no. She returns to her former position, and sobbing more bitterly than ever, rests her head upon the rock.

It is wonderful, also, that Mary does not grieve so much because Jesus is dead, as because the body is removed from the tomb, and she believes his enemies have carried it away. Had any one asked the weeping woman to explain her feelings, she would have confessed that her sorrow had been more bearable while she believed the beloved corpse to be resting in the tomb, although she could not explain wherefore. And can we not sympathize with this feeling? Do we not all know the unutterable woe, far worse than the first pang of separation, which we experience when the dead body of him whom we love is borne from our door, never to be viewed by us again until time shall be no longer? Or was the sorrow which troubled the heart of Mary occasioned only by the removal of the corpse, which prevented her showing her love and veneration towards it, by anointing it and strewing it with spices? O, it was far, far more than this! True, she was unconscious of entertaining a thought of the resurrection; but, though unconsciously, this thought still lurked in her heart. Many things pass through our minds which we are far from comprehending clearly; is it not then possible that there might be sounding in the secret chambers of her soul an indistinct but half-understood echo of the mysterious words which Jesus had uttered concerning the raising up of the Temple in three days; and also of the Son of Man having to pass three days and three nights in the heart of the earth, as Jonah did in the whale's belly? Love hopeth all things, although it may be unconsciously; and Mary would certainly have understood her own feelings had any one thus addressed her: "Magdalene! the dove-like eyes of thy blessed Lord are forever closed; that mouth, from which flowed to thy wounded heart the balsamic stream of heavenly peace, will never more open to address thee; those feet, so beautiful on the mountains, will never more tread this vale of tears; and that true and faithful heart will beat no more, for it is now the prey of corruption!" Then, I can answer for it, Mary would have ceased her weeping to reply to those unworthy sentiments, and with energy she would exclaim, "No: that cannot be; it is impossible! Eyes like these may sleep, but could not be extinguished; and a mouth like his may rest, but could not be silent and dumb for ever!" We should now perceive with astonishment how faith loves, and love believes, and how hope still continues, although all probability of joy and happiness has departed.

How often do we meet with similar occurrences in Zion! How often do we behold souls sorely tempted, who obstinately maintain that Jesus has forsaken them, that he loves them no longer, and will never confess them in the presence of his Father—in short, whose firm conviction is that they are lost! Offer them consolation, and they reject it: point out to them the promises in the Bible, and they say they can lay no claim to them. But suppose that we change our tone for a moment, and with solemnity exclaim, "Alas! alas! we fear you have no part in Christ Jesus!" Their language instantaneously alters; with the most impressive earnestness they deny our assertion; and from the dark background of those hearts, which appeared at first in such utter despair, we behold the light of hope dart forth like lightning, and maintain the field against all the temptations of the adversary.

III. Mary now stooped down to look into the sepulchre, for she could scarcely believe that the beloved corpse was actually away. What then did she perceive? O miracle! Yet it is only we who cry, "O miracle!" Mary joins not with us; for what she perceives brings no change to the feelings of her heart. She beholds two forms of light sitting in the tomb—two angels, one at the head, the other at the feet, where the body of Jesus had lain. It almost appears incomprehensible how she did not conjecture that their appearance had some connexion with the removal of the body. In the persons of the two angels there shone forth, if we may so express it, two bright rays from the Easter sun; and yet she will not understand that it is Easter. Never before had seraphs abode in the graves of the dead; and in this case the grave honoured the angels, and not the angels the grave. One might suppose they sat in the most glorious temple earth could offer; such silence and solemnity breathes around, they are sunk in such holy contemplation, and their countenances express such sublime devotion. Their thoughts are, "Here slept the Lamb of God! Here lay the only-begotten of the Father, who died for sinners!" And even those glorious angels are oppressed by the sublimity of those conceptions. They cannot turn their eyes away from the place where the body lay, and they sit as though it were still there; one at the head, the other at the feet, thus giving us to understand that it is still their centre; the point around which the circle of their thoughts and feelings revolve, and the unsearchable mystery into which they desire to look.

It is not merely from choice that the angels sit in the tomb of their Lord; he himself has commanded it, to assist his weeping lamb to discern what has happened, to dry her tears, and enable her to understand that her Master now commands a thousand times ten thousand, and has exchanged his garland of thorns for a kingly crown. And certainly those blessed spirits esteem it a glory and an honour to serve one favoured by such a king, and to bring her the first intelligence of the most blessed occurrence that could happen to sinful man. The very circumstance of their sitting within the open tomb, is in itself a gospel enlivening the soul; for is it not one of the most blessed fruits of the resurrection? Henceforward the graves of the saints have a different aspect; they are sleeping chambers, silent, but not gloomy; angels of peace watch around them, and the brilliancy of the morning of the resurrection penetrates even their darkness.

It is strange that the sight of those two forms of light makes no impression upon Mary: she sees, indeed, that they are angels; but does Mary seek angels? No, she seeks Jesus; and her heart is so bowed down with sorrow that even the presence of the angels is insufficient to bring her the least consolation, for the mournful images which so rapidly pursue each other through her agitated soul, leave her no time to reflect or take rest. The blessed spirits excite neither joy nor alarm in her bosom, for her soul has been so shattered already, nothing new can move it, and her sorrow is of a kind which even angels cannot alleviate. Leaving the heavenly visitants unnoticed, she continues to weep; and never before were they so little regarded by mortals as by the sorrowing Magdalene.

When the angels beheld that the mourner took no notice of their bright and shining forms, they opened their mouths, and with unspeakable kindness and love thus addressed her: "Woman, why weepest thou?" What did they mean by this question? To find out the cause of her tears? O no! that they already knew. The question, "Woman, why weepest thou?" was the expression of their astonishment at beholding on the most joyful morning which ever dawned upon earth, the sinner bathed in tears, who, above all others, should appreciate the joy of that incomparable day. They, inhabitants of heaven though they were, might well envy the circumstances of this sinner, and, if it were possible, wish to exchange with her: glad to give their treasures, for her treasures, their righteousness for her righteousness, and their heaven for her heaven: and yet Mary weeps inconsolably! They see the Prince of Life approaching from the distance, to prepare for her such a blessed Easter as has never since been solemnized on earth; they see him about to present to her as an Easter-gift the whole fruit of his death and resurrection, and about to lavish upon her all his loving-kindness and compassion; and yet Mary still weeps as never woman wept before! O that they were permitted to tell her how unutterably happy she ought to be! But no, they must be silent, for their Lord has so commanded. Therefore they express all that they are permitted to say, in the question, "Woman, why weepest thou?" In other words, "Is it possible that thou canst weep? This is no longer the time for sorrow! Weep no longer, for the

Lion of the tribe of Judah has overcome—and thou in him—eternally!"

Has Mary no misgiving when she hears this question addressed to her? Does it tell her nothing—and can she not read the Easter message in the joyful countenances of the angels? No, no: Mary comprehends, Mary anticipates nothing. She only hears an inquiry concerning the cause of her woe, and replies in broken accents, "Because they have taken away my Lord, and I know not where they have laid him." "Whom, Mary?" "My Lord," is her answer; and well may she so name him; dead as she believes him to be, he is still her Lord and her King, her all, and the ruler of her heart! Day and night he hovers before her eyes, and is the centre of her thoughts and feelings, her love and her solicitude. The world finds no part in her, for she is engrossed entirely by him: his bloody image she preserves in her soul as an all-powerful magnet, and uses it constantly to influence her goings out and comings in, to enable her to choose the good and refuse the evil. "My Lord!" said Mary. Is it her troubled heart that thus speaks? No, no: far in the depths of her soul there sits a beautiful angel, who, without her being aware of it, comforts her more than the angels who are visible, and to him the wonder is, that she has not altogether despaired. It is the angel of hope; nevertheless we must confess, that she herself has no idea that such an angel hovers amid the gloomy clouds which overshadow her heart; she continues to sob and to weep, for she thinks that despair is her portion.

IV. But why do we grieve any longer for Mary's tears? They are indeed superfluous; it would be far better were she to smile and rejoice, than to weep; and although she is still enveloped in night and darkness, yet the Easter sun is already ascending the heavens, and the objects of woe and terror which she beholds exist nowhere but in her own imagination. Beyond that gloomy scene which her faint-hearted melancholy presents to her eyes, the world is bright and beautiful, like the Paradise of old; and had she only entered the garden one short half-hour before, she would indeed have ceased to weep—she would have seen the Holy One, and been a witness of his resurrection, which took place, as you are aware, in the early morning dawn. The tomb had been silent and closed until then; the King who had been slain, lay amidst the spices in the deep slumber of death; and the guard who kept watch rejoiced along with the Prince of Hell, because the third day had now appeared, to annihilate for ever the dream of the Galileans concerning the resurrection of their Master. Even while Satan was calling to his dark companions, "Brethren! the reign of the Nazarene is over!" the hour of the eternal Father arrived; the angels sang with joy to the music of their harps, and a seraphic pair stood ready behind the clouds to dart down at the first signal to the silent garden. What happened? The Father spoke. Borne by the breath of life which proceeds from his mouth, the voice of the Almighty penetrated the gloomy vault of death. The words, "Awake, my Son! in whom I am well pleased!" pealed and reverberated over the dead. The bowels of the earth now begin to tremble —the ground shakes as though the world were about to fall in pieces—the rocks burst asunder; an angel, shining as the light, appears at the tomb, grasps the ponderous stone, hurls it from the door of the sepulchre, and ——— Ha! what is this? They who keep watch fall to the ground, like dead men; a cry of terror penetrates even down to hell; but the heavens rejoice! Who is it steps out of the gloomy chamber? Who is it before whom the heavenly beings bow down? To whom do they pay homage, as their Lord and their King?——It is he, it is he! Jesus, the crucified one! He was dead, and yet lives! He has gained possession of the field, he waves the flag of triumph, and bears the keys of hell and of death!

This, then, my brethren, was the glorious occurrence which took place very early on Easter morning. Mary as yet knew it not; we however know it, and rejoice with great joy on account of the stupendous miracle. To those who are convinced, that without a pledge and mediator they would be utterly undone, it must always be the most important question, "Whether Jesus continued to lie in the grave, or rose from the dead?" All is staked upon the inquiry, for Jesus could not have been the Christ had he remained in the imprisonment of the tomb. What should we have thought of the man who had assured us he should rise on the third day, if death had continued to hold him captive? of the man who had undertaken to conquer hell and the grave, if he, on the contrary, had been overpowered by them?—of the man who had declared, "I and the Father are one," if the Father had seemed unconscious of it, and regarded him no longer?—of the man who had promised to save his people by offering up himself as a sacrifice in their stead, if God had refused to accept him, and permitted him to rest in all the ignominy of a shameful death? We should have regarded him as put to shame, and all his labours branded as useless; and such a saviour, or to speak more correctly, no saviour, would the poor sinner have found in Jesus had he remained in the grave. The disciples felt this bitterly, and for this reason the time between the Friday of Passion week and the Sunday morning was the most sorrowful, and at the same time the most terrible, in the whole period of their existence. But what joy when the message was delivered to them, "Christ is risen!"

In an instant the fallen palace of their hopes was raised up from its ruins, more glorious and more beautiful than ever, and resting now upon adamantine foundations. No, no, my brethren, we can never mistake, we can never be in error, while we rest upon Jesus as the rock of our salvation; the Easter miracle assures us that we build our hopes on the right person; no one can henceforth say that we relied upon a man who could not keep his promises. Certainly when his words came to pass, "Destroy this temple, and in three days I will raise it up!" we may well, henceforward, rest implicitly upon his truth; and no one can say that we trusted in a man who is not the Son of God. His triumph over hell, death, and the grave, and the majesty with which he steps forth from the tomb, casts the last doubt with regard to his divinity to the ground, and inscribes with gigantic letters on the book of history, "This is the true God, and in him is everlasting life!" No one can any longer despise the grounds on which we build our trust; for does not the Eternal bear witness to their stability, by not merely summoning our dead Lord from the tomb, but clothing him in such glory and brightness? Does it not prove that God not only takes pleasure in the work of his Son, but that it is a work perfected and completed, in which sinners may securely find refuge? Yes, let us take fast hold of our Immanuel, and build on him the glorious temple of our hopes; knowing that we stand upon a rock which the waves of doubt may assail, but which they can never shake.

V. Let us now look back to Joseph's garden, and behold our King coming forth in the silence of the morning, beautiful and glorious as the orb of day. Earth has never seen him in such splendour, nor yet have the heavens; the rising sun does him homage, and the world is like a paradise, over which a morning-star has just arisen. Lo! there he is approaching, but O how different, how very different from before! No crown of thorns now encircles his head, no garment of mockery envelopes his limbs; but the splendour of the diadem glitters on his brow, the Glory of God covers him as with a garment, a heaven of joy can be read in his glance, and the salutations of peace are on his lips. How peacefully and how gladly can we now rest our eyes upon him! No longer does he say, mysteriously and sadly, "Whither I go, ye, cannot come." Nor yet, "I have a baptism to be baptized with; and how am I straitened till it be accomplished!" But he says, "I come into my garden, to eat of my own fruits!" And now we may apply to him the words in Genesis, "He couched as a lion, and as an old lion; who shall rouse him up?" His soul now enjoys the most ecstatic delight, that of Easter: the joy which had been promised him, and for the sake of which he had suffered death on the cross, is now realized; and in the consciousness of the reconciliation being accomplished between God and man, it seems as though he bore paradise about within his own bosom; and the thought that a sinful people have been purchased and redeemed by his blood, penetrates and flows through his soul, like a river of delight, fresh from the fountains of heaven.

The countenance of the Father, so long hidden from his view, now shines down upon him in all its loveliness and splendour; and the belief in his love is now changed into the vivid consciousness of its reality. The fulness of those blessings comprehended in the expression, to rest on the bosom of the Father, is now restored to him; and though the gates of heaven are not yet opened to admit the Prince of Life, and though the thousand times ten thousand, with their golden harps, have not flown down to meet him, and to cast their crowns at his feet; yet it is only because we poor children of the dust would be almost annihilated on beholding such pomp and glory, as never entered our feeble imaginations to conceive, and instead of drawing near to our Mediator, we should then have required a new one to enable us to approach him. Yes, my brethren, all is so silent around, and Jesus, instead of being clad in a starry mantle, is still clothed in the garment of humanity, in order that sinners like us may form such a picture of him in our hearts, as we can comprehend, and that we might draw nigh with a good courage unto our Lord and our God.

Had it not been for this, all would have happened differently in the garden of Joseph, and one scene of glory would have succeeded another. Well might the holy angels feel, that here for once sinners might take precedence of them in singing Hallelujah; for the Prince of Easter bears a far more close relation to us than to them. It is we whom he has snatched from the depths of hell, and not they; it is we whom he has drawn out of depths of destruction, in which they were never plunged; it is we whom he has released from the curse, while *they* have never experienced what it is to be rejected of God; we have been clad in the garments of his righteousness, while they have never stood in want of it, having never been poor and weak and helpless. In short, although Jesus may be the source of joy and delight to the angels, yet they can never possess what we possess in him: he is ours, as he is no others'!

VI. Bathed in tears, Magdalene is still standing before the open grave; suddenly it seems as though she were not alone, for she fancies that she hears footsteps. In alarm she hastily turns her head, but perceives no one on either side; now it occurs to her to look behind, and—who is he whom she beholds? Only

Joseph's gardener;—at least so she believes, and sobbing leans her face once more upon the rock. O, it is touching and heart-moving! His breath touches her head, his image is reflected in her tears; one step only is between her and rapture; but how little is she aware of this, she who only beholds one abyss after another opening before her! The supposed gardener, who is even now preparing to work in his garden of mercy, to raise up the trees thrown down by the storm, and to refresh the languishing flowers with the dew of Easter joy,—this gardener now opens his mouth to the weeping woman, and with friendly accent addresses her in the words of the angel, "Woman, why weepest thou?" This question is the first which has been uttered by our Lord since his resurrection, and is indeed addressed to all his people. The words, "Why weepest thou?" if they did not dissipate at once the clouds of sorrow which overcast Mary's soul, must at least have broken them, and prepared her in some measure for the scene about to take place. She needed some preparation, otherwise she could not have borne the surprise, and would almost have died from the excess of her wonder and joy. The gardener continued, "Whom seekest thou?" This question also contributed to fan the little flame of hope in Mary's heart, and enticing it forward from the back-ground in which it had been hid, made the mourner conscious of its existence. "Sir," she replies, "if thou have borne him hence, tell me where thou hast laid him and I will take him away." Had the gardener not known already how much her heart was bound up in the beloved corpse, he might have gathered it from her present words. "If thou have borne him hence." *Him*, whom meanest thou, Mary? Oh! surely all the world must know whom she means! The gardener has only to say where the dead body is lying; and no matter where it may be, or what danger and toil she may have to endure, she will go and take it away!—But the gardener is silent.

VII. Mary continues to weep, abandoning herself totally to her grief; and now the Saviour thinks there has been enough of mourning, and that it is time for her to hold her Easter. That which now happens, my brethren, you must imagine for yourselves: it is not for me to strive to adorn the simple narrative of the Evangelist with the flowers of speech, or to depict a scene which indeed far surpasses the power of human description. Two words only were uttered; one by our Lord, and the other by Mary. This is the whole scene; but the hearts which overflow in these words, the holy rapture which they enkindle, the ocean of joy and love which they comprehend, the heaven of peace and delight which they disclose;—these are what are indescribable! The glowing pen of a seraph would not suffice to do them justice. But why do we say seraph? for a pardoned sinner could far better venture to attempt it. Mary weeps; suddenly she starts as out of a dream! What is this? she is called by name. "Mary!" resounds in her ears, and a cold shiver runs through her limbs. But why is this? She hears a voice which sounds like *his* voice; it was in these tones, in these soft accents, he used to address her.

Trembling she looks around;—into the grave, but *there*, there is no one;—on her right, but she beholds nothing. "Can it have been the gardener?" And as she thus thinks, she turns round and looks upon him;—she looks, and looks again—yes, yes, it is the gardener! —O Mary, compose thyself! collect thy thoughts, and sink not altogether under the weight of thy surprise! —She sees in the gardener Him who was dead, but who now lives! and once more she beholds her lost paradise; for the man who brings salvation, and who is the realization of her dearest hopes, is now restored to her! Her poor heart sinks under the weight of such overwhelming emotion! She falls down, her feet give way, her knees can no longer support her, and she breaks forth into a cry of mingled tenderness, devotion, astonishment, and rapture, "Rabboni! my Lord and my God!" My brethren, ask me not to describe this scene; all is comprehended in the heartfelt exclamations, "Mary!" and "Rabboni!" and language can add no more. If we say that when Mary heard her name pronounced, it seemed to her like a vessel richly freighted with Easter consolation sailing towards her, and was a seal and pledge of her eternal safety and happiness, it will but give a faint idea of what the word "Mary," as uttered by our Lord, expressed. We may with confidence say that Magdalene, now a blessed saint in heaven, still remembers the joyful moment when the Prince of Life beside the empty tomb called her "Mary!" and when the angels strike their golden harps, she still thinks in her heart, "Sweetly as this sounds, it does not sound like

'Mary!'" Yes, in order to comprehend all that this little word expressed, we must have seen the glance with which our Lord accompanied it; the eyes of unutterable grace and compassion with which he looked down upon her; the sunny splendour of love which shone in his glorified features, and the heaven of salvation and joy which beamed from his countenance;—we must have heard the sweetness of the tones in which he spake, and felt the wafting of the breath which accompanied his words;—these, and many other things, we must have beheld and experienced, ere we can have the faintest idea of what the word "Mary" was, as uttered by Jesus risen from the tomb. And the reply of Magdalene, "Rabboni!" who can fathom the depths of *its* meaning? Words would fail to describe the joy which is expressed in it, the devout astonishment, the unutterable tenderness, and the full and free giving up of the heart which accompanied it: it seems as though, notwithstanding all our endeavours, we never could penetrate beyond the surface of the deep thoughts and feelings which are comprised in the one little word "Rabboni." There are sounds which seem echoes from the realms of eternal life, which awaken in the soul a longing for its home above, and blissful conceptions of a futurity beyond the grave; but these sounds cannot be expressed in human words. The Saviour rejoices because his work is now completed; while the lamb of his fold rejoices because she is once more near him, and is assured of peace and salvation; and she inquires no more concerning either earth or heaven, because *he* has been restored to her who transforms every place which he enters, into a paradise. It is as though one had dreamt that he stood on the brink of the sea, watching the progress of a little vessel which contains all he holds most dear—wife, children, and friends. Suddenly a storm arises; the waves of the sea roar; the little vessel totters and capsizes; it sinks into the abyss, along with all that is contained in it. This is the man's dream; and the scene takes place so vividly before him that he believes it to be reality. With a cry of terror he awakes, and trembling looks around him; when lo! he beholds all his treasures unharmed; he becomes aware that it was only a gloomy vision which alarmed him; a feeling of gladness takes possession of his heart, and he shouts and rejoices.

Thus Magdalene felt, only unutterably more happy; for the vessel which she had believed shipwrecked, bore still more precious treasure than these; and now it was all restored to her, and the blissful past, which she for a while believed to be lost for ever, had returned. The happy woman now knew to whose standard she had sworn allegiance; for since Jesus lived, it was clear as day that he was the Son of God, and the Lord of heaven. All that he had promised had come to pass, and had even now received the seal of its truth; and at the same time the bright palace of her peace and her hope had risen up from its ruins more beautiful and more glorious than ever, and now rested upon imperishable and adamantine foundations.

VIII. At the moment when Mary falls enraptured at the feet of Jesus, he utters the mysterious words,

"Touch me not; for I am not yet ascended to my Father: but go to my brethren, and say unto them, I ascend unto my Father, and your Father; and to my God, and your God." The expression, "Touch me not!" has a depth of meaning which we cannot fathom: perhaps our Lord made use of it to quiet the storm of emotion in Mary's bosom, and to show that henceforward he would not stand in his previous human relation to his followers; perhaps also to prepare her for the time when she should no longer know him after the flesh, or behold him personally, but when she should see him with the eye of faith. Yet, my brethren, ye must all feel that these explanations are but imperfect, and do not penetrate beyond the surface of these mysterious words.

The command which follows is more intelligible, and at the same time is unutterably consoling: "But go to my brethren, and say unto them, I ascend unto my Father, and your Father; and to my God, and your God!" From those words bursts forth a splendour, shining upon those whom the Lamb has purchased with his blood, such as has never illuminated even the world of angels. No, never did the Lord of heaven approach more closely to his redeemed: he names them as his brethren—what honour and glory! "I ascend," he says, "unto my Father, and your Father; and to my God and your God." Was not this joining himself, the only-begotten Son of God, with poor sinners, in one dignity, in one perfect man, before the Lord? Thus we see how he knows them no longer after the flesh, but regards them in an Easter light, in the splendour of the perfected reconciliation. He judges then according to what he has done and performed for them, and, as their Head, beholds them receiving those tokens of fatherly grace and love which were due to himself. These words of Jesus disclose to us, likewise, that side of the Easter miracle which may be designated the most glorious and the most blessed. Here, as in one radiant focus, the beams of its splendour are collected together: may we never lose sight of them; but always rejoice, henceforth, in the glorious union of the Son of God with the brethren, and name Easter in future as the day of *our* honour and triumph, the day when *we* received the crown of immortality!

Is not this a glorious history? Confess that you have never heard its equal! Say, could imagination conceive any thing more enrapturing? These scenes however, were not described to gratify our sense of beauty; but to raise up our hearts to heaven, and to breathe into our souls eternal life: they form the first links of a golden chain of circumstances reaching down to the present hour. Yes, even now there is no want of occurrences in the midst of us, similar to those which happened on the first glorious Easter morn. Many sorrowing and almost despairing souls hear their names pronounced, as Magdalene did of old, and by the same gracious lips; and many a "Rabboni!" is uttered by those who are shedding tears of joy. The Lord is indeed nigh! he manifests himself to all; and his Easter salutation resounds through our souls, while rejoicing we reply, "Amen; blessing, and glory, and wisdom, and thanksgiving, and honour, and power, and might, be unto our God for ever and ever. Amen."

THE WALK TOWARDS EMMAUS

LUKE XXIV. 13—34

And, behold, two of them went that same day to a village called Emmaus, which was from Jerusalem about threescore furlongs. And they talked together of all these things which had happened. And it came to pass, that while they communed together, and reasoned, Jesus himself drew near, and went with them. But their eyes were holden, that they should not know him. And he said unto them, What manner of communications are these that ye have one to another, as ye walk, and are sad? And the one of them, whose name was Cleopas, answering said unto him, Art thou only a stranger in Jerusalem, and hast not known the things which are come to pass there in these days? And he said unto them, What things? And they said unto him, Concerning Jesus of Nazareth, which was a prophet mighty in deed and word before God and all the people: and how the chief priests and our rulers delivered him to be condemned to death, and have crucified him. But we trusted that it had been he which should have redeemed Israel; and beside all this, to-day is the third day since these things were done. Yea, and certain women also of our company made us astonished, which were early at the sepulchre; and when they found not his body, they came, saying, that they had also seen a vision of angels, which said that he was alive. And certain of them which were with us went to the sepulchre, and found it even so as the women had said; but him they saw not. Then he said unto them, O fools, and slow of heart to believe all that the prophets have spoken! Ought not Christ to have suffered these things, and to enter into his glory? And beginning at Moses and all the prophets, he expounded unto them in all the Scriptures the things concerning himself. And they drew nigh unto the village, whither they went; and he made as though he would have gone further. But they constrained him, saying, Abide with us; for it is toward evening, and the day is far spent. And he went in to tarry with them. And it came to pass, as he sat at meat with them, he took bread, and blessed it, and brake, and gave to them. And their eyes were opened, and they knew him; and he vanished out of their sight. And they said one to another; Did not our heart burn within us, while he talked with us by the way, and while he opened to us the Scriptures? And they rose up the same hour, and returned to Jerusalem, and found the eleven gathered together, and them that were with them, saying, The Lord is risen indeed, and hath appeared to Simon.

It is wrong, my brethren, to praise one part of the word of God as if it were better than another. The Scriptures are everywhere good and beautiful, and exalted far above our criticism. Every branch of the tree of life affords a whole harvest of heavenly thoughts, which if we do not gather, the fault is our own. Nevertheless, there are places where the golden fruit appears richer and more plentiful than in others, but particularly in the section which we have just been reading; for the first glance at this part of the gospel awakens the whole sympathy of our hearts. Our interest increases the longer we contemplate it; it delights and enraptures us, while it irresistibly chains our attention, for a whole heaven of blissful ideas is comprehended in this glorious narration. Let us now consider more nearly each single trait in this beautiful gospel, but particularly in the manner in which the disciples journeying towards Emmaus became aware of the resurrection of Christ; and let "Life illuminated by the light of Easter," be our theme.

I. It is between afternoon and evening; the sun is now about to set—and surely it has seen glorious things this day. Two men are walking on the lonely mountain-path between Jerusalem and the village of Emmaus; two artisans, if one may judge from their appearance. One is Cleopas, probably the brother-in-law of the Virgin Mary; the name of the other is not mentioned. What if he were Nathanael, the Israelite without guile? It is uncertain though very possible. They belong to the followers of the Nazarene; not to the twelve, but most probably to the seventy; at any rate to the persecuted brethren. The sequel of the history proves that they were not even men in Christ, but children after the Spirit; nay, perhaps not even yet regenerated. We must on no account imagine that the followers of our Saviour, generally speaking, were heroes of the faith, or masters in Israel; on the contrary, they did little else than try the patience and exercise the long-suffering of their Lord on every occasion. For example, one petitioned to sit at his right hand when he should ascend the throne of David; another, following the blind dictates of his affection, attempted to prevent him accomplishing the work of reconciliation, and strove to hinder him going to Jerusalem to fill the office of our great high-priest. On another occasion they run towards him, transported with joy, like simple children who have learned some new feat of dexterity, because they can now drive out evil spirits, and perform miracles. Again, they are impatient for the day when their Master should expel his enemies from the land, and when they, filling the highest offices and inhabiting the most splendid dwellings, should become partakers of his majesty and glory. Nay, at times such childish acts and follies come to light, which have been committed by the disciples, as might almost make us believe they had not been at the time converted and regenerated. But whether this were the case or not, their names at present have long stood recorded in the book of life, and they themselves have long enjoyed the sunshine of their Saviour's love.

The two disciples, journeying towards Emmaus, seem indeed to have been but children in the faith, and do not appear to have looked deeply into the mysteries of the cross. In wisdom and knowledge they are poor, but they love the Lord Jesus from their hearts; and fire is there, although as yet it may not have burst forth into light.

One can gather from their appearance that some calamity has newly happened. Alas! they are indeed very sorrowful. Their minds are disquieted with questions and doubts, while their hearts are heavy with grief and vexation. True, they are walking on a pleasant mountain path, surrounded on all sides by the blossoms and verdure of spring, while the birds are singing, some in the air, and some among the branches; but the joyfulness of nature harmonizes ill with their feelings. Their brightest hopes, their most cherished projects, and their sweetest dreams, have been buried in the grave with Jesus. What is their Christianity now, and on whom can they pour out their love, since they have no Christ? Their Lord is dead. Did he even lie in the grave, they would know where all their hopes and joys were buried; but alas! they have been in Jerusalem, and found the tomb desolate and empty! What then has become of the beloved corpse? To how many conjectures may not the circumstance of its disappearance give rise! The women who spake with the angels that were sitting in the tomb, related strange things which they had said. But what angels? Hope and love are apt to imagine many things, and therefore the women prove nothing. Why did Peter see no angel when he visited the grave? And why did John, the beloved disciple, who lay on the bosom of Jesus,—why did he behold nothing? Alas! we need no longer hope; all is over with our cause, and there is nothing more to expect! "Yet," says the one to the other, "might we not hope a little longer? can we? dare we? Cleopas, suppose for a moment that the women had actually beheld angels, and that they said he was alive! If this were the case!—Cleopas! If—if—but—" Alas, this *but* occurs again; they are afraid of deceiving themselves, those poor disciples; and therefore they embrace the doubt more firmly than the hope. They now proceed on their way: thought after thought crowds into their minds, producing a wild confusion; yet they cannot come to any certain conclusion. Now fear and now hope predominates; then they are terrified at their own presumption, and resign themselves to grief anew. How earnestly do those two pilgrims converse! even at a distance one can hear of whom they are speaking. Verily, the cause of their Lord and Master is dear unto their souls; and whatever faint-heartedness and unbelief they may be accused of, God will assist them in his own good time, and the good seed which has been sown in their hearts shall certainly come to light.

Our Lord does not always approach his people, when

he is about to convert them, in the same manner in which he approached the two disciples. Suddenly, and like an armed man, he comes to many; arresting them in the midst of their godless life, while surrounded by the temptations and allurements of the world, and softening in one instant their cold and hardened hearts; the first symptom of their conversion being a cry for pardon and mercy, and an earnest desire to be cleansed in the blood of the Lamb. With others, our Saviour acts in a more silent and secret manner, employing gradual manifestations and long preparation. As, when winter is just past, we derive more delight, if possible, from the unfolding of the leaves, the budding of the flowers, and all the sights and sounds of early spring, than from the warmth of May and the luxuriance of summer; so the eye of an experienced Christian derives a similar pleasure from contemplating the first symptoms of divine grace in fallen man; for he regards them as blossoms, which promise a future harvest of rich and beautiful fruit. Yet the commencement of this work of grace is often to all appearance trifling and unimportant, and we frequently see nothing which can be termed repentance or contrition; nevertheless, there is a secret disquietude in these souls, and a feeling that the great thing requisite to their happiness is awanting. Although there may be no supplication for grace and mercy, there may be a heartfelt longing for a glorious treasure which they know not how to name;—no bold acknowledgment, "Thou art the Christ, the Son of the living God!" and yet an earnest inquiry after their Redeemer, and the things of his kingdom ;—no solemn oath of allegiance to the banner of Zion, no decisive step towards joining the people of God ; and yet a devout attention, when the gospel is spoken of, an earnest endeavour to walk in the right path, a longing to attain certainty in their religious views, and an unwearied search after truth and peace. You must not expect, however, that a man of this description will join with you, as you would wish, in lauding and magnifying the Saviour, and praising the miracles of his grace and mercy. It is quite possible that he may feel uncomfortable in the midst of you, and be silent and dumb in your society; and this, not from enmity to your holy cause, but because he is secretly grieved that he cannot express himself like you, and that while you mount on eagles' wings almost farther than his eye can reach, he is forced to remain grovelling upon earth. Nay, you must not even be astonished though he should gainsay your opinions, and exclaim with Nathanael, "Can there any good thing come out of Nazareth?" For probably the same honest desire to find out the truth may lurk in his soul, and the next day he may cry out with the same fervour, "Rabbi, thou art the Son of God; thou art the King of Israel!" And were he to enter an assemblage of mockers and blasphemers, I can answer for it, that though he might previously have withstood you, on this occasion he would take the part of the gospel, and loudly and unreservedly confess that Lord whom he himself has not yet found: nay, he will even confess more than he actually believes and is conscious of, for his heart whispers, though it may be but faintly, that it is truth which he contends for. When we meet people such as I have just described, we may well yield to the dictates of that love which hopeth all things; like friends and brothers we must accost them, and on no account condemn them for their wavering and unbelief, lest we vex that Holy Spirit, who is even now working within them, and whom it pleases on this occasion to bring forth first the blade, then the ear, and afterwards the golden corn in the ear.

II. Sorrowful and utterly cast down, the wanderers pursue their path; alas, what an Easter have those poor men kept! It is a pity that they have left Jerusalem so quickly, but this cannot be altered now: had they remained there only one short hour longer, much grief and lamentation might have been spared them, for then they would have heard from Mary Magdalene what wonderful things had taken place. Unfortunately, however, they had departed from Jerusalem at the moment when the joyful life of Easter began. Thus men frequently stand in their own light: but beware of doing so, ye among my friends who are still mourning and weeping, and whom the Easter sun has not yet illuminated: be not too hasty in deciding what has taken place, or what must be done. Resist this tendency to rash measures, for it is evil; close not your heart against hope, but give heed when you hear its little voice whisper, "Jesus lives, and I along with him! The Lord is risen indeed!"

The farther our two pilgrims travel from Jerusalem, the heavier do their hearts become. Alas! their oppression and sorrow is so great that they seem even to breathe with difficulty; though at times a spark of hope arises in the bosom of one of them, it flickers upwards only to be extinguished by the doubts and objections of the other. If the one ask whether it can be possible that *his* cause is lost who commanded the winds and the sea to obey him; the other shakes his head with a sigh, fearful of exciting hopes in the mind of his friend which must end in bitter disappointment. Again and again they repeat over to each other the late mysterious occurrences; at intervals some word of promise shines in the back-ground of their memories, only to die away the next moment, and their countenances change colour, brighten and are overcast with gloom, varying like their thoughts, their opinions, and their feelings. The end of their discussion, however, is always the same: "Yes," say they, "our sweet dream is over, and our life of sorrow has begun—may God take pity upon us!" Unfortunate men! beaten and harassed by the storm, it seems as though the sun would never shine upon them again. And yet who is there that would not like to stand in their place? Who would not gladly exchange all earthly splendour for the happiness which is even now awaiting the wanderers? O sorrow without cause, and unnecessary grief! We may compare them to a man who is living a twofold existence, and who at the same moment breathes in two worlds, the one of which resembles the other as much as the darkest and most cheerless night does the brightest and loveliest day. And certainly the world in which our disciples imagined themselves to be at present was like a night-scene, in which neither moon nor stars are visible in the heavens, and darkness which can be felt is covering the land. Here they were poor, forsaken children, with neither father nor mother, sinners, with none to save and none to help them. O what a world of misery and confusion! A world where nothing can be seen before them, and where the hand of Providence cannot be traced; a world where the raging lion goes about, with none to stay his ferocity; a world under the government of the blindest chance, groaning under the curse, and ruled by the sceptre of the king of terrors, from whose destroying power none can make their escape,—not even the Immaculate One, the Lord of Heaven! A gloomy House of imprisonment for lost and hopeless creatures; one vast abode of sorrow, suffering, and death; the gloomy ante-chamber, opening into eternal desolation, and the terrific preparation for hell!

Such was the aspect of one of those worlds in which the two disciples were existing. And what was this world in reality? A mere dream of the imagination; a delusive picture mirrored in their faithless hearts. They breathed at the same moment the air of a different world, clad in different colours, illuminated by a different light. It was the new world which commenced in the early dawn of Easter day, and which was born while the heavens were thundering, the rocks were splitting, and while the morning stars were shouting for joy;—a world of splendour, triumph, and glory, where the raging lion is trampled in the dust, and where the king of terrors is disarmed and dead;—a world from which the curse has been removed, and which is gladdened by the smiles of the Almighty; where the angels of God are constantly descending upon errands of mercy, and upon whose throne a Prince of Peace is wielding his gentle sceptre. Yes, it was a world such as this which surrounded our disciples; but how little were they aware of it! Obstinately they remained in the gloomy dream which the timidity of their hearts and their want of faith had created, instead of entering the joyful light of the Easter world, which shone so gloriously around them. Nothing more was necessary than that some friendly hand should come to their assistance, and open the windows of their souls, in order that they might see clearly. What beautiful objects would then meet their gaze? In an instant the voice of their complaining would cease, and the clouds of their sorrow be dissipated like the mist of the morning by the rising sun. Already this hand is approaching the wanderers; and in a few moments more the darkness of their dream will be dissipated, and the joy of Paradise and the light of the Easter world will dawn in their souls.

III. We shall now leave the two pilgrims for a while, as another and more glorious object arrests our attention: it is the person who appears at some distance, walking along the same path. Who is this Stranger? Do you not know him? It is—it is the Easter King! Let us sing Hosanna to greet him! But before approaching him more nearly, I must relate his history. He, as you are aware, was from all eternity in heaven. What induced him to snatch sinners from destruction, I know not, for the word *love* says too little, and raise them to the glory of heaven. For this purpose, when the fulness of time had arrived, he descended to this earth amid the songs of the blessed angels, and took upon him our nature. He became a man like unto us, with the exception of our sinfulness; for sin had no part in him, although he took it upon himself. It was ascribed to him as though he, the Holy One, had committed it; and like us, he stood before the tribunal of God, charged with the same transgressions, and condemned to undergo the same sentence.

While he was thus standing as our representative, he said, "I go to the Father!" thus designating his pilgrimage through this world; and certainly it was a most wonderful thing that he, in the character of our Pledge, should be going to the Father. It was a thing in which we, as sinners, were inexpressibly interested; for should he attain this goal, should he actually be received into fellowship with the Father, then it was clear as day that there would no longer be any hindrance in our path to heaven. Our Saviour, as being laden with the burden of our sins, was to be treated like ourselves; if then the Father's arms were opened to receive him, it would be a certain proof that they would also be open to receive us. But what happened? Scarcely was this mysterious journey towards his Father's house commenced, when a mighty difficulty arose. The word "Stay!" was thundered forth, and a voice cried out from the throne of the Majesty on high, "They alone are permitted to enter my sanctuary who have kept what is written in the book of the law!" The great Pilgrim heard—but did he turn back? No: he gave due honour to eternal holiness, subjected himself to the law, and by his perfect obedience removed the hitherto insurmountable difficulty which lay in our path to heaven. Amid a thousand trials and temptations, he fully satisfied the demands of the law, and presented such a righteousness to the eyes of his Father, that the latter cried out from heaven, "This is my beloved Son, in whom I am well pleased!" "I go to the Father!" said this wonderful Man once more; and in truth we had reason to hope that he would be able to penetrate to the heart of his Father, and along with him that we should also; for he acted in our name. But, alas! once more the word "Stay!" was thundered from the throne, and the same voice pronounced the words, "A late obedience will not suffice; sins which have been done cannot be undone; and the sentence which has been uttered must be put into execution!" Our great Pledge replied, "I am ready to suffer it!" Then the heavens began to lour, the sword of vengeance was unsheathed, and the lightnings flashed from the clouds. His path now led to the gloomy garden of Gethsemane, then ascended the terrible mount Golgotha, and ere we were aware, the martyred Lamb lay bathed in his own blood. "It is finished!" were his own words from the cross; but no, heaven was not yet satisfied. A third time the word "Stay!" was thundered forth; and instead of the arms of eternal love being stretched forth to receive him, a terrible monster opened his frightful jaws to engulf him.

He died by a fearful death, and his bloody corpse, instead of being received in the paternal arms, was cast into the dark and gloomy grave. Then did he fail in reaching the longed-for goal? Certainly, while he lay in the tomb he had not attained it; and if he were not to succeed in reaching heaven, and softening the heart of his Father, then, alas! nothing was more certain than that we also must be for ever separated from God, and that at the close of our pilgrimage we must become a prey to a hateful death. For it must not be forgotten that Jesus in our name sought the path to his Father's house, that he stood in our place, represented our persons, and that in looking upon him we must regard him as being one with ourselves. His fate was therefore our fate; and while he was dead, and lay in the ground, rejected and forsaken by God, alas! our cause did indeed look terrible, and no star of hope and consolation shone through the dark clouds of our existence.

But lo! who is it that now approaches? A much desired and most blessed object! Yes, yes, it is He! the Pilgrim who suffered death! Let every heart rejoice! Let every breath be a Hallelujah! What a heaven of blissful hope, what a paradise of peace and joy, discloses itself to our view in the reappearance of our Lord and Brother! Yes, he has reached the goal; he has found an entrance into his Father's house! Joy, joy, for us! We now rest in the arms of eternal love, and our path loses itself in the splendour of the great Easter morning; for the person of Christ contained ours, and what he did has been done by all his people. Now we behold him approaching in the light of his new and glorified existence: the Father has loosed him from the bands of death, and showered down upon him riches and blessings. Jehovah has by the resurrection of his Son proclaimed aloud his fatherly approbation, and testified in accents of thunder that he is worthy of the glory of heaven, and that all power and dominion are his due! How nearly does this testimony concern you poor sinners! For you it was uttered! to you it was given! and you it was whom the Father on the third day received to his heart! O remember that it was not Jesus alone, but you also in whose place he stood, whom the gates of heaven opened to receive! You conquered in the garden of Joseph, you were pronounced justified, you found the path to the heart of the Father, and upon your heads descended those sunbeams of divine mercy, with whose splendour you behold Jesus clad this day!

IV. The two disciples are still sorrowfully pursuing their path, when a third person comes up behind them. "Where two or three are gathered together in my name, there am I in the midst of them." They have no idea who the Stranger may be, and they trouble themselves about it as little, for they have no desire for companionship. The Unknown meanwhile redoubles his speed, and approaches nearer; when he gets up to them he salutes them, and appears as if he wished to join their party. Ah! did they but know who it is that greets them! Meanwhile they regard the Stranger with curiosity, and measure him from head to foot with a hasty glance; but no, his face they never beheld before; he is certainly a stranger, probably returning from the feast. They now resume their discourse, after returning his salutation, for they trouble themselves about him no more. The pilgrim, however, remains, and almost forces himself upon them. And does he not always do so to those who receive him upon earth? We now behold the two disciples walking side by side with the Unknown. Go on in peace, ye pilgrims! for ye have with you the cloudy pillar, and the pillar of fire; the rock which Moses struck, and the bread from heaven! But they still perceive nothing, for their eyes are closed. My brethren, there are many among you who resemble them; the same Man accompanies you, walking side by side, often for a long time before you recognise him; although afterwards, I grant, in looking back to the thousand circumstances which then took place, you exclaim with Jacob, "Surely the Lord is in this place, and I knew it not!"

The stranger now addressed the two pilgrims: "What manner of communications," said he, "are these that ye have one to another, as ye walk and are sad?" Thus unlocking their hearts as though with a golden key, that all might flow out. Is it not generally the case that he commences his wonderful operations in the heart of man by asking a question? And when such a question is asked, is not silence at an end, and does not the answer seem to come of itself? But when does Jesus ask this question? When the heart is so full and so heavy that it seems as though one could no longer support it; when one feels that there is no one to understand him, and still less one to help him. Then upon your knees ye must speak to the invisible God, and pour out your inmost soul in his presence: you must say *all*, *all*, for Jesus himself questions; he asks you what ye have been talking about on the way when ye looked so sad; and our Lord knows so well how to ask, that one can lie for hours prostrate before him, and yet always find more and more to say to him, ever remembering something else which ought to be confessed, until at length his whole heart has been poured out. People frequently think that they act thus of their own accord; but they are mistaken; the voice of an invisible Being draws them on, until all gives answer; the mouth with words, the eyes with looks and tears, and the heart with sighs. And yet it is a frequent question, "Does God hear all that we say?" My brethren, how can *he* fail to hear, who knows so well how to ask?

Now I shall tell you how our disciples replied to the question of the Unknown. Cleopas answered, "Art thou only a stranger in Jerusalem, and hast not known the things which are come to pass there in these days?" The Stranger really appears not to have heard of these occurrences, and asks, "What things?" They must now relate the history to him, although he knows it already far better than they do; for where he addresses a soul in an earnest manner, that soul must reply to him frankly and fully. In such a conversation it will not do to speak in general terms, such as, "I have sinned, O Lord!" Nor yet must we reckon on his omniscience to excuse the poverty of our confessions, saying to ourselves, "Why should we particularize our backslidings, when he knows them already better than we do ourselves?" No, this does not satisfy Jesus: "What things?" he asks our hearts again; and does not permit us to rest until we are circumstantial in our confessions, and until we unveil before him the inmost secrets of our bosoms.

When their unknown Companion demanded "What things?" the two began to relate them. Oh! did they but know who the person was to whom they were relating his own history!—"The man," say they, "of whom we have been talking, and on whose account we are so sorrowful, is Jesus of Nazareth, a prophet." What! ye faithless ones—a prophet only? Have ye not heard this prophet say, "All men should honour the Son, even as they honour the Father?" Have ye not heard his testimony, "He that hath seen me hath seen the Father;" besides all that he said concerning his Godhead?—They lauded him as a prophet mighty in word and deed, and as a man true and holy in all his ways. Yes, they had been convinced of this, but, alas! the mighty words they had heard from him had now lost their force, and his deeds had not corresponded to their expectation.—"The chief priests and our rulers," continue they, "delivered him to be condemned to death, and have crucified him." It was this circumstance which proved their stumbling-block. Oh! why had they not better studied the 53d chapter of Isaiah, the 22d Psalm, the 13th chapter of Zechariah, the allegories contained in the sacrificial ceremonies, and the raising up of the brazen serpent? They now go on to say, "But we trusted that it had been he which should have redeemed Israel." Thus we perceive how they knew nothing of what had taken place on the third day: and because the Lord had not yet appeared to them, his words with regard to his own resurrection went for nothing.

They then relate how certain of the women had visited the sepulchre early in the morning, and thrown the disciples into alarm by their intelligence that the body of the Lord had disappeared; and how they had also beheld a vision of angels who told them that Jesus was alive. Alas! why had they not believed this message, which might have saved them all their doubt and suffering! But their own blind reason, and not the word of the Lord, reigned supreme in their hearts, banishing obstinately all idea of the resurrection of the dead.—"And certain," continue they, "of them which were with us went to the sepulchre, and found it even so as the women had said; but him they saw not." These are the words of the two disciples; they mean well, and they say what they believe. It is evident that they still love the Lord Jesus with their whole heart, and still, in spite of their blasted hopes, rely upon him; but the torch of their faith burns dimly, and their thoughts are a melancholy confusion of folly, prejudice, ignorance, and blindness. They have ceased to look to the Scriptures, they have forgotten the words of Moses and the prophets, and have rejected the testimony of their Master. This is their own misfortune; and their words, "But we trusted that it had been he which should have redeemed Israel," show the secret cause of all their grief and trouble.

Who had told them to expect a temporal redemption and a temporal kingdom at present? Why had they not regarded the words of Jesus, when he said, "My kingdom is not of this world?" And why had they not examined more diligently Moses and the Prophets? "But we trusted!" Truly, even in the present day, this is the cause of many of the tears which flow in Zion. People make a Saviour out of Jesus according to their own wishes; they say he must do so and so with us; and what they wish for, they expect. When it happens otherwise, they sigh and lament, exclaiming, with the two disciples in our history, "But we trusted!" Yes, continue to trust and hope, my brethren; but hope according to Scripture, and cast anchor on the firm ground of the Word; if you do so, the heaven of your lives will not be overcast. The whole narration of Cleopas confirms what we said before with regard to their ignorance and want of faith; nevertheless, we behold sparks and flames appearing at intervals, which cannot let us doubt that the Holy Spirit is even now working in their hearts. How freely and unconstrainedly do they confess in the presence of a stranger, their dependence on the crucified One! And certainly to make this confession in those times of danger, a greater courage was required than flesh and blood could give. What tender love to the dead do we discern in the attempt to raise him above all criticism and all condemnation! And how touching and important is the circumstance, that as far as they comprehend the glory of their Master, so much do they strive to weave a crown of splendour which may encircle the head of the dead! This is also manifest in their secret hope that they may win the Stranger to the cause of Jesus; and gain him, deceased though he be, a new disciple in the person of the Wanderer. Does not this trait in their characters enable us to perceive a hand-writing, such as nature alone could not have traced in their souls? and do we not inhale the fragrance of a flower-bed of thoughts and feelings such as the heavenly Gardener alone could have planted?

V My brethren, do ye not begin to understand the reason why our Saviour delays to open the eyes of the two disciples? Say, would it have been to their advantage had he disclosed himself to them at once? I think not. Amazed and thunderstruck they would have stood before him, but without knowing the cause of the reappearance of their Master; and without having the least idea of the true meaning and consoling efficacy of his resurrection. Probably they would have felt as their brethren afterwards did, in that well-known evening hour, when they would not trust the evidence of their bodily eyes, that it was Jesus who stood in the midst of them; but were terrified and affrighted, supposing they had seen a spirit, or a visitant from another world, instead of deriving peace and gladness from his presence. Had they even been convinced that it was in reality their Master whom they beheld, and that he indeed lived again, still his presence would not have assured them of what they ought to have been assured. But perhaps you think they would have rejoiced, and said among themselves, "The sacrifice which Jesus offered has been accepted by God! God has pronounced us blessed in him, and absolved us from our sins! We have risen from the dead along with him; we have been exalted, justified, and declared worthy of heaven!" You are indeed mistaken; as yet they have not the least idea that Jesus suffered in their stead, and delivered them from their sins upon the cross; for they who cannot understand Christ crucified, cannot understand him risen from the dead. We cannot sufficiently admire the wisdom of Jesus in closing their eyes until he had expounded the Scriptures, and proved that the Messiah must suffer and die; showing then the importance of his rising from the dead, bursting open the prison of the tomb, and stepping forth, crowned with honour and glory.

Scarcely have the two disciples finished their sorrowful narration, when the unknown One raises his lance to chase away the spectre which is even now attempting to pour the fiery poison of despair and unbelief into their hearts. *Faithlessness* is the name of this monster. Our Lord makes use of words sharp and cutting, like a two-edged sword; and in this the wisdom of that Man was seen, to whom his enemies bore testimony that he spake as one having authority. "O fools!" he begins, "and slow of heart to believe all that the prophets have spoken!"

Yes; the bitter medicine of an earnest reproof, especially if it be mingled with love, penetrates to the heart more quickly, and enlivens the faith more powerfully, than even unalloyed compassion, or friendly consolation. A sentence such as this uttered with authority,

"O fool! thou dost desire and long for Jesus; why then dost thou not call to mind his words, 'Blessed are ye that hunger now, for ye shall be filled?'"—or, "Ye faithless ones, who know that ye are in Christ Jesus, and that ye belong to him! why do ye let the consciousness of your sins torment you? Why do ye doubt and make that scripture a lie, which says so plainly, 'There is no condemnation to them who are in Christ Jesus?'"—words such as these are often of mighty service, and resemble the soft and enlivening breeze, which, after a storm, is wafted over hill and valley to refresh the weary and weather-beaten wanderer. Suppose a man who has cause to reckon himself among the poor in spirit and the heavy-laden, but who, at the same time, is conscious of being the child of God; if such a one pursue his appointed path sighing and lamenting, instead of rejoicing, does he not merit reproof, and not commiseration? and is not the root of his grief to be found in the slowness of his heart? Such a fool stands in his own light; and it would be better for him, if, instead of cherishing his melancholy fancies, he would read the Bible, and constrain his obstinate heart to believe the promises which have been given him: certainly it is not for him to choose whether to accept them or not; whether to allow or deny their efficacy.

It must have made a singular impression upon the two disciples, when the Stranger, from whose lips they expected to receive compassionate sympathy, began all at once to reprove them, and chide their unbelief. I can imagine them looking in astonishment at one another, as much as to say, "What does this mean? Who is this man?" They are struck dumb, and cannot understand it: meanwhile the sharp and cutting words of the Stranger act like a whirlwind in dispelling the clouds of their grief, or like lightning illuminating their spiritual night, and changing in an instant the whole frame of their minds. The strange Pilgrim continues, "Ought not Christ to have suffered these things, and to enter into his glory?" And now he begins to prove it out of Moses and the Prophets, thus opening to them the holy place of the ancient manifestations of God. He leads them through the beautiful garden of the divine promises; enables their spiritual ear to hear the voices of the old seers and prophets joining in one mighty chorus through all the ages of the world; accompanies them through the various pictures, shadows, types, and figures, which refer to the mysterious sufferings of Christ; and shows them how the great God of their fathers had borne testimony from the beginning of time to the foundation of his Son's kingdom by the shedding of his blood. He then unfolds to them the grounds upon which the Messiah must suffer, in order to redeem the world; and explains to them the mystery of Christ being our great High-Priest and Representative. He speaks of Jesus taking upon himself the debts and obligations of sinners; of the perfect obedience which he presented to his Father in the name of transgressors; and of the full satisfaction which he offered to eternal justice, by subjecting himself to the curse, and undergoing a fearful punishment.

After he has thus gradually brought to light the necessity of the sufferings of Christ, he comes to the glorification of the Redeemer—reminds them of the text which refer to his resurrection and ascension—and unfolds before their eyes the great document attested by the Father, in which it is declared, that the Son has, by the sacrifice of himself, made ample satisfaction for the sins of the whole world. He shows them from the mouths of the prophets, how our great Pledge must rise out of the dust of humiliation; how the Father must recal to life the mighty dead—crown him with glory and honour before the eyes of the world—and thus confirm his mediatorship, proclaim the perfection of his work, justify him, and declare him to be worthy of his promised reward. But he also enables the disciples to look still more deeply into the mystery of the glorification of their Redeemer; he teaches them to view it, remembering that Christ is their representative; shows them that his Justification and being crowned with glory is of value, not merely to himself, but to those sinners in whose place he stood; and explains the mystery of their being risen again, exalted, and glorified along with him.

Thus, my brethren, our Lord led the disciples through the midst of those gospel truths, as a shepherd leads his flock through the most nourishing pastures. Meanwhile they cannot account for what is happening to them, and think they never before heard any one speak with such power, depth, and clearness. Astonished, they look at one another, then measure their companion again with their eyes, as though they had some misgiving of the veil which enveloped him, and would gladly, if they could, pierce through it. A very little more would make them fling their arms, with tears of joy, round the neck of this wonderful man; but then again such awe and veneration overpowers them, that they almost prostrate themselves at his feet. "O Cleopas!" says the one to the other, "If I did not see him, and if I only heard him speak, I should think he was our Master; for he who illumined our souls with such sunbeams, and whoever kindled such fire in our hearts, but the incomparable One, whose loss we now mourn?" Each moment their souls become clearer and brighter; the mist of their prejudice and erring conceptions is dispelled, and star after star shines forth in what had previously been utter darkness. As their hearts burn within them, their courage rises, their withered hopes once more become green, and the prospects around them brighten. Their sensations indeed cannot be described; it seems as though a curtain were rolled away from their eyes, disclosing a new world, and as though they heard harmonies and heavenly melodies such as their souls could not even have imagined. "And must he indeed have suffered!" say they in their hearts; "Did he stand in our stead, and take upon him the weight of our guilt! Then all that which passed at his death was necessary, and agreed with the eternal plan and counsel of God, as manifested in the Scriptures! Only the proclamation on the part of the Father were then wanting, that the Son has perfected his work. There is still one link which we miss, in the wonderful chain of events that have taken place for our salvation, and that link is the last—the resurrection and glorification of our Representative. But what if this also has really taken place; for has it not been proved to us that it must necessarily follow? If Jesus should prove to be already crowned!—indeed it is quite possible; for the woman may have spoken the truth; and it may have been the herald of Christ's triumph who accosted him at the grave. Cleopas, suppose he should suddenly appear to us,—the living and the glorious One!—O happiness! We should then be free of our cares for ever; we should be raised from the dead, and exalted in the person of our Master, and then for the first time be conscious of all we possess in Jesus!" Thus, my brethren, glimpses of light such as these may have darted a fleeting illumination through the hearts of the two disciples. Without the twilight of the Easter world was beginning to dawn in their souls, and made them happy once more. If Jesus had now appeared to them they would indeed have known all they possessed in him; they would no longer have regarded him as a phantom, or as a mysterious appearance, but as a man whom they knew and understood, for they now would view him in the clear and brilliant light of the sure word of prophecy.

VI. "Did not our heart burn within us, while he talked with us by the way, and while he opened to us the Scriptures?" These are the words in which the two disciples afterwards described their sensations, while listening to their unknown companion. And, my brethren, have not we also felt this burning of the heart, while our Saviour has been visiting us? His tongue is like a lance of fire to probe our inmost souls, and sparks and flames issue from his lips. Do you not remember how for a time we went about hungering and thirsting, not knowing well what we sought, and being unable to describe the good which we wished to reach? Then Jesus came and accosted us, but we knew not that it was he. He said unto us, "Why are ye so grieved and cast down?" while at the moment that he questioned us he helped us to answer; he showed us the state of our own heart, explained the nature of our vague longing, and then declared to us the words of Moses. Do you still remember how he led us around Sinai and Ebal? The mountains of the law were enveloped in clouds; it thundered and lightened, and the voice of the great trumpet penetrated our very souls! It was then he told us of his Father, that he was all-holy, and terrible as a consuming fire. What a sermon that was! We beheld the King of kings upon his great and glorious throne, and we trembled before him. When he uttered the first low whisper concerning our sins, how heavy and sorrowful we became—sorrowful as we had never been before! And when he then began to explain the mystery of the cross, and to unfold the Scriptures, how the scales fell from our eyes! We felt as though the fragrance of flowers were wafted around us, and as if the portals of the clouds were opening, disclosing to us a new and blissful world of light. Oh! how much have we yet to relate concerning those important days, when our Lord first began to teach us when he first whispered to our souls, and in gentle accents strove to awaken it from its sleep of death! We knew not then who it was that spake with us ; we sat at the feet of a Gamaliel, but how great a one we little knew.

How can we describe the feelings which we then experienced! Well may we exclaim with the disciples, "Did not our heart burn within us, while he talked with us by the way?" Yet some have felt this burning of the heart in one way, some in another. One may describe his feelings in this manner: "At that time it seemed as though I solemnized the christian festivals in my soul. It was Christmas; I beheld the Babe lying in a manger, and with my spiritual ears heard the angels singing; then I bent my knees with the wise men; but I only did it partially, and did not prostrate myself in the dust. My heart burned within me, and there surely was a prayer in my soul; but I knew not yet how to worship the Child; I required first to become a child myself. I now beheld our Lord's passion: I was in Gethsemane during the awful night; I did not sleep with the disciples, but watched with the Redeemer, heard his prayers, and beheld his sufferings. When he exclaimed, 'O my Father, if it be possible!' how my heart burned within me! I perceived a great mystery, but the key was wanting; for I was not yet regenerated. Still I could not let the cross out of my sight; and it was clear to me that he was more than a prophet, more than a martyr, and more than a hero, who now died for truth. My heart burned while on Mount Golgotha; and I could almost have cried out with the centurion, 'Truly this man was the

Son of God!' and gladly, had I had courage, would I have exclaimed with the dying thief, 'Lord, remember me when thou comest into thy kingdom!' I then walked in Joseph's garden on the third day, beheld the rocks burst asunder, and saw the Conqueror of death issuing from the tomb. O how my heart burned within me?—I perceived more than a gardener!—I called out, with Magdalene, 'Rabboni!' But I did not say with Thomas, 'My Lord, and my God!' No, I was still unable to do so; for though great anticipations of Easter stirred through my soul, they were indistinct and uncertain. The Easter world lying before me was still enveloped in mist; nevertheless there was a vague and half-understood voice whispering in my heart, 'Here, little bark, tossed upon the stormy waves, thou mayest cast anchor!' Then I went to the Mount of Olives, and beheld the Lord of glory ascending into heaven. Never before had my heart burned within me as it did now; I felt as though I had wings, and were ascending also. Heavenly Magnet, it was thy first and all-powerful attraction; still I did not anticipate that of which I am now certain, that thou wilt one day actually take me along with thee! I then solemnized Pentecost, and the burning of my heart was but an unconscious longing for the fulfilment of the promises that we should pass from death unto life, receive the dew from on high, and that the Spirit should descend upon us!" This then is the way in which some may describe the budding and germing of their spiritual life.—Now let us return to our two wanderers.

VII. Our disciples, have reached their goal, and

Emmaus lies before them. How short has their three hours' journey seemed!—Still engaged in the most interesting conversation with the Stranger, they are about to turn into the peaceful little village, surrounded so beautifully with vine-covered hills; when suddenly their companion stops short, and seems about to take leave of them. "How!" say the disciples, "mean you to go farther?—indeed this must not be!" Their hearts are already bound up in this man, and they cannot bear to part with him; if he go, it seems as though he would carry their very souls along with him. They had felt on the road that if he were not their Master, he was at least his living picture, and in looking at him they seemed to behold the twilight dawn of their risen Lord's approach. His conversation, in its effects upon them, resembled the rosy glimmer of the morning red, which, before the sun is visible, gilds the highest points of the mountains, and though not the sun itself, yet announces the approach and the speedy appearance of the king of heaven. Their hearts live already in an Easter world, although with fear and trembling, for they do not dare to allow themselves wholly to believe it; and the question whether they are awake or dreaming is not yet decided; though it must be so should this wonderful Stranger remain.

We now see these two agitated men standing before him, and holding him back with their hands. "No!" say they, with the utmost earnestness, "thou must not travel farther to-day: remain this night with us! Dost thou not see it is already evening, and the day is far spent; therefore remain, remain! If thou goest, then, alas! we shall sit down again in despair, and mourn and weep anew. On the contrary, shouldst thou remain, how happy we should be in our intercourse with thee, and how wonderfully consoled! for we are certain thou canst tell us more about Christ, and dispel the clouds from our souls. O then, remain! Although we have only an humble cottage, yet remember thou art welcome! surely love will make up for all that is awanting!" Thus spoke the two disciples; and much more would they have said, had they expressed all that they felt in their hearts. They are tied to the mysterious Stranger by inexplicable chains; and it is only when they seem about to part that they begin to feel them.

Let us now look back to our own journey towards Emmaus, at the moment when our unknown Companion asked us, "Wherefore are ye so sad?" and when we were enabled to reply through our tears, "Lord, we mourn for our sins!" Our situation then resembled that of the disciples at the gate of their little city; with both hands we held him back, and besought him with prayers and tears to remain. "But it is not merely, "Remain with us!" that we say! it is, "Come, Lord Jesus!" And how much does the word "Come!" express, when the long dream of our own righteousness and strength begins to be interrupted, the day of our natural security and peace with ourselves is about to close, and the evening of sorrow is overcasting the soul! The words, "Come, Lord Jesus!" will then neither permit us to slumber through the night, nor be silent during the day. On the wings of desire our souls seem to arise from amidst the tumult of life; and waking or sleeping, we cease not to stretch out our hands towards our Saviour. Oh! how impatient does this little word "Come!" sound, and how perseveringly do we utter it! We weary not, and nothing can terrify us, or make us silent: boldly it penetrates the clouds, and stops not until it has attained its object. When this word "Come!" is repeated again and again in our hearts, it is as the voice of a new life; and where the cry is heard, "Come, Lord Jesus!" then indeed the day is far spent; already it is evening; and soon may we expect the morning when the sun will appear.

VIII. The Stranger now accedes to the request of the two friends. He will then remain. "O Cleopas!" cries Nathanael, "this is indeed most glorious! What an evening we shall spend!" But Cleopas is already away; he has run on before, to announce the arrival of a guest in his cottage, and to prepare for him a friendly reception. The Guest follows with Nathanael, and is welcomed with the most heartfelt joy at the door of their humble dwelling.

It is the hour of the evening meal; a simple repast is served, and the Guest is invited to partake. They go to table, and the Stranger takes upon himself the duties of the master of the house. "Formerly," think the disciples, "our beloved Master did the same;" and sorrowful reminiscences pass through their souls. Their Guest now rises from his seat, and they along with him. How often did their Lord stand thus in the midst of them! He raises up his eyes to heaven in the attitude of prayer. Thus Jesus was accustomed to look to his Father! The Guest begins to pray. "My God! what voice is this?" He breaks the bread: the disciples gaze at one another in astonishment. "Cleopas, where are we?"—He reaches it to them. Wherefore now do ye not take it? Cleopas! Nathanael! are ye both in a dream? Ye seem not to know whether ye are awake or asleep. Who is it that is standing before you? Who is the man that is now offering you bread? Look at his countenance;—is what ye see real, or is it a deception? "Ah! it is indeed his face!—these are his eyes!—Look, Cleopas, look!—see how clear and distinct it is becoming!—his heavenly features!—and the wounds on his hands!—he smiles to us!—O heaven!—It is indeed He!—It is our Lord, risen from the dead?" Now, indeed, those happy ones at length see clearly;—there he stands, beautiful, in his Easter glory, in the full splendour of his triumph,—of his new and immortal life! Trembling and pale, from mingled emotions of astonishment and joy, the disciples stand for some moments fixed and immovable; gazing upon him as though they would impress his image in their souls for ever. Then their knees begin to shake, and they prostrate themselves in the dust, to worship the all-glorious One, and cover his feet with their kisses and their tears of joy; when suddenly, like the lightning which darts from the clouds and as quickly disappears, the beloved form vanishes from their eyes: but the heaven of peace and happiness which he disclosed to them still remains behind in their hearts, and the Easter sun has risen upon them in all its splendour.

My brethren, scenes similar to those which took place in Emmaus happen daily in Zion; for the joy of Easter did not terminate along with the forty days. Oh! what delight we experienced when Jesus suddenly unveiled all the sympathy and love of his compassionate heart to our weeping eyes! What happiness in those evening hours, while we believed him afar off, when suddenly we heard the salutation of peace issuing from his beloved lips, when he comforted our timid souls, and when we distinctly heard him say, "Fear not, I have redeemed thee, and called thee by thy name, for thou art mine!" When God enabled us to behold our justification in his perfect sacrifice of himself, to reckon ourselves among those blessed ones who are born again into everlasting life, to rest upon the bosom of Jesus, and to cry with the Psalmist, "My soul shall be joyful in the Lord: it shall rejoice in his salvation!" then was there a repetition of the scene at Emmaus; and that heaven which disclosed itself to the two disciples was manifested also to us. It was to this goal that the words, "Come, Lord Jesus!" led us; and who is there that does not wish to hear this "Come!" sounding in his heart?

IX. The two disciples are transported with wonder and joy; sobbing they fling themselves into each other's arms, and can scarcely find speech, so great is their emotion. "O Cleopas!" cries the one, "who could have thought it! Happy, happy are we that we have seen him again! But how did we not sooner recognise him? Is it not wonderful that the burning of our hearts within us did not betray him, while he talked with us by the way, and expounded to us the Scriptures?" No, ye pilgrims, it was not wonderful: men are always more sharp-sighted and more acute, on looking back to what is past, than when it has been happening. The words, "Surely the Lord is in this place, and I knew it not!" have been repeated a thousand times in the lives of Christians, when they first beheld the light of eternity streaming across their appointed path, and dissipating its gloom.

We can easily perceive why our risen Lord so quickly withdrew himself from the eyes of his happy disciples. They were not henceforward to live in the enjoyment of his human presence; on the contrary, they were to exist in those blissful conceptions which his speech and conversation had caused to enter their hearts. They now knew all that they possessed in their blessed Master, since his resurrection from the dead. It was not vague anticipations and indistinct emotions which his re-appearance excited within them; on the contrary, it was bright and glorious ideas raising them up to heaven. They had lost a beloved Friend and Master, to find him again as a pledge and representative with the Father. It was a Prophet mighty in word and deed whom they had laid in the grave, to be restored to them on Easter day as a great Head, with whom we, the members, are joined together in one perfect body. In Him they beheld themselves raised from the dead, justified and glorified; and a nearer intercourse with him in his early human form might have prevented them viewing him in this spiritual light, and weakened their consciousness of the mysterious union between him and themselves. Had he remained with them, they might have retraced their steps from the glorious point of gospel illumination which they had now attained, to the lower one of knowing him only after the flesh; and in the excess of their joy at beholding him near once more, they might have forgotten that mystical connexion between them, the contemplation of which formed their happiness and peace. Their Lord had only appeared to them in order to convince them of the reality of his resurrection; henceforward they must live in Christ as their Representative and their Head, and not view him as such with their bodily eyes, but with the eyes of the Spirit, and by means of faith.

The happy disciples meanwhile have left us; borne on the wings of joy, they rush along their mountain path, until they reach their brethren at Jerusalem, to astonish them with their glorious intelligence. Happy, happy pilgrims! well may they be termed blessed! But whosoever envies their joy, let him remember that their history is not an isolated and extraordinary occurrence; on the contrary, it is but a picture of what happens in the lives of many Christians. The Man who accosted the wanderers, and joined them on the way, is no other than he who gave us the assurance, "Lo, I am with you alway, even unto the end of the world!" Although Emmaus may have disappeared from the earth, yet thousands of similar places have been made by the words of Jesus, "Behold, I stand at the door and knock: if any man hear my voice, and open the door, I will come in to him, and will sup with him, and he with me!"

O then may this history become our own experience, and may the past be transformed into the vivid present! Let us not content ourselves with the enjoyment which the contemplation of these Easter scenes afford. They are not mere objects to delight the eye; on the contrary, they are symbolical pictures, delineated over the portal of a new and more glorious time, expressing deeply, yet significantly, the manner in which Jesus acts upon the souls of his chosen ones. They were not formed merely to be retained in silence in the chambers of our memory and imagination; no, they were intended to exercise an influence upon the whole circle of our feelings and experiences. After looking upon them, we must turn our eyes upwards unto Him, who is as near to us as he was to the two disciples on the mountain path; and we must cry, "Lord God of our fathers! accompany us also this day!" When this ejaculation mounts to heaven on the wings of faith and love, we do most surely receive an answer. Then each house among us becomes like the cottage at Emmaus, and each heart is a temple of Easter peace; the festival is never-ending, and we cry out, enraptured, "The Lord is risen indeed!—Hosanna in the highest!"

EASTER PEACE

Luke xxiv. 36—46

And as they thus spake, Jesus himself stood in the midst of them, and saith unto them, Peace be unto you. But they were terrified and affrighted, and supposed that they had seen a spirit. And he said unto them, Why are ye troubled? and why do thoughts arise in your hearts? Behold my hands and my feet, that it is I myself: handle me, and see; for a spirit hath not flesh and bones, as ye see me have. And when he had thus spoken, he shewed them his hands and his feet. And while they yet believed not for joy, and wondered, he said unto them, Have ye here any meat? And they gave him a piece of a broiled fish, and of an honeycomb. And he took it, and did eat before them. And he said unto them, These are the words which I spake unto you, while I was yet with you, that all things must be fulfilled, which were written in the law of Moses, and in the Prophets, and in the Psalms, concerning me. Then opened he their understanding, that they might understand the Scriptures, and said unto them, Thus it is written, and thus it behoved Christ to suffer, and to rise from the dead the third day.

This is a well known and frequently studied history; and well may it be so, for it is full of deep import and contains a fund of instruction. Let us now principally direct our attention to the pains taken by our Lord to remove the doubts and fears of the disciples, and to enable them to contemplate the day of his resurrection with joy and gladness. We shall also say a few words upon the subject of Easter peace; consider all that is signified by the word *peace;* then that which hinders many Christians from enjoying it; and, lastly, in what manner a path is prepared for its entrance into our hearts.

I. The great day of the resurrection is now drawing to a close; it is already night; and we find ourselves in a room surrounded by the disciples. Here Easter peace is breathed, but only by a few: the two disciples from Emmaus enjoy it; Magdalene also, and Simon. The others are wavering between fear and hope, and many are still sorrowful, for they cannot help regarding the story of their Master's resurrection as a fable and a delusion. They believe that Jesus is dead, and that he has only been carried away by his enemies; thus their hearts find no consolation, for the assurances of their Master, from which alone they could have derived it, seem to have been put to shame. "Now we have no shepherd," say they among themselves, "no protector, no guide, no representative!" And they are like to sink to the earth with grief and sorrow, when they think, "We are weighed down by our sins; we are surrounded by a thousand adversaries; the grave lies before us, beyond that the judgment-seat, and hell is in the distance!" They strive against those terrible thoughts, but without effect, and in such thoughts there can be no peace. Anguish possesses their souls, and the little bark of joy is far away, tossed on the ocean of doubt.

The disciples are sitting together in a close circle, eagerly conversing, and in rapt attention, listening to the oft-repeated story of the brethren from Emmaus. The door of the house, as well as that of the chamber, is locked, for they are afraid of being interrupted by the Jews. But what is this? Suddenly they hear a voice in the midst of them, "Peace be unto you!" Pale with terror, they spring from their seats, and—what do they behold? Who is he that stands in the midst of them? They believe they see a spirit,—an apparition from another world, and a cold tremor creeps over them. We, however, behold our beloved Lord and Saviour, for it is indeed he, and no other. The object for which he comes has been unfolded in his salutation—he comes to bring peace to his children! This had been his employment even early on the morning of that day, and it remained so as long as he tarried upon earth. But what manner of peace is this of which his little flock are to become partakers? It is indeed a wonderful, an inexhaustible, and a glorious peace! Not a peace such as the world can give and take away; but such a peace as Jesus himself enjoys,—his own peculiar Easter peace; for his own words are, "Peace I leave with you; my peace I give unto you!" Invaluable treasure! Let us now contemplate it more nearly.

It is a deep and unutterable peace. Look at the Saviour, as he stands before us after his resurrection; how serene and joyful he appears, and what a halo of sabbath stillness surrounds him! No where can we perceive a trace of care or sorrow; the days of weeping are past; the complaint is no longer heard, "My soul is exceeding sorrowful, even unto death!" And the cry, "My God, my God, why hast thou forsaken me?" having broken forth once from his lips, was never to be uttered again. All oppression and heaviness have been removed from his soul, and darkness and woe have disappeared. His heart resembles a calm and tranquil sea, in which the constellations of heaven are reflected; his mind is serene, like the bright morning of a festal day; and his spirit is a holy temple, filled with harmony and love. His bosom is a fountain of peace, and it is this peace which he brings to his sheep, this Easter joy which he now offers them.

But is our Saviour entitled to give away this peace? Is it well grounded and does it rest upon foundations of adamant? While on the cross, when he bore our curse, and the weight of our sins, he did not possess this peace; there he suffered and languished in torment: but now he hangs no longer on the accursed tree; the Father has raised him from the dead, glorified and exalted him; pronouncing with a voice louder than thunder, "There is no more guilt resting upon him—he is spotless, he is righteous, and worthy of a throne of Glory!" I now hear the wise of the earth saying, "that it is clear the Saviour must enjoy peace, but that it is impossible for a sinner to do so, since, where it exist, there must also be that from which the peace of Christ takes its rise, namely, a consciousness of having performed the will of the Eternal Father, and merited his love." In so far they are right, and speak wisely; but not the less do I cry unto them, "Ye fools, and slow of heart, will ye never comprehend?" It is necessary for us to feel a twofold consciousness, and we must regard ourselves as being, like Christ, justified and well pleasing in the sight of God. But are ye astonished at my words? and are ye inclined to reply, "No! it would be sinful and wrong were we to think of ourselves so highly!" Alas! my brethren, it is your blind and foolish reason which will not permit you to enjoy peace; for I maintain that that man can never possess it, who is unable to say, from heartfelt conviction, "Jehovah loves me!" Nor can any one believe that the God of holiness loves him, until his conscience bears testimony, "Thou art justified, thou wast obedient, and thou hast performed thy obligations!" The Bible, however, expressly assures us, that the peace which was enjoyed by Jesus risen from the dead, may flow into our souls also. It is written, that "in Christ we are made the righteousness of God;" in other words, giving us the assurance, that as the Father loves Christ, he loves us also who are the members of Christ. Thus we are called to the enjoyment of the peace of Christ, deep and perfect, such as the Prince of Peace himself enjoys, and resting upon the same foundations; for in him we perfected the work of the Father, and through him merited Jehovah's approbation. Do ye now comprehend why our Saviour accosted his disciples with the salutation, "Peace be unto you!"—why he stretched out his hands, and desired them to look upon his wounds? It was virtually saying, "Well may ye enjoy peace, since I have fulfilled the demands of eternal justice for you!" And does not Paul also say, "Who is he that condemneth? It is Christ that died, yea rather, that is risen again, who is even at the right hand of God, who also maketh intercession for us." Yes, it is Christ, who, in dying for us, bore our curse,—in whom we have risen from the dead,—are justified in the sight of God,-- and pronounced worthy of his parental love!

The peace of our risen Lord is glorious and triumphant; it sustains every proof and every trial; and all that assails it must infallibly be dashed to pieces. It withstands the law, for Jesus supports it; it overcomes the grave, for "Grave, where is thy victory?" Even death does not shake it; for Christ dies no more, but bears the keys of hell and of death: and it looks unmoved upon the judgment-seat, for we are blameless through the merits of the Son of God. Can Satan harm it? No; Jesus has overpowered and vanquished him. Is it moved by the fiery terrors of the last day? No; for Christ is the Judge of the quick and dead. "Yes," ye reply, "all this may be true; but I have yet to die;—I have yet to meet the powers of darkness;—I stand yet upon the field of combat. How then can that peace which Jesus enjoyed dwell in my heart at present?" Thou fool, listen to the words of the apostles, who were still alive when they said, "No, we are dead!" Were they terrified on approaching the night of the grave? Far from it; they gloried in having risen along with Christ. Did they wish first to vanquish Satan? That thought was far from their minds; for they beheld him lying bruised and overcome under their feet. Did they suppose that they must not rejoice until they had attained their goal?

Not so; they beheld themselves there already; for they knew that He was powerful and true who had called them to his inheritance. They were as peaceful and joyful as though they sat already upon a throne of blissfulness in heaven, and beheld the world and the devil—death and the grave—lying far beneath their feet; for they knew that if not to-day, they should at least sit there to-morrow, as surely as their glorified Representative had done before them. Thus they enjoyed even then the perfect Easter peace of Jesus, and rejoiced in his glorious resurrection.

II. Could our Saviour have left behind any thing more desirable than the cup of his Easter peace, out of which he himself had taken the first draught, and which he in his salutation, "Peace be unto you!" bequeathed to his chosen for an eternal possession? This cup of joy is even to this day passed from one to another in our christian communities; but how few there are who taste its contents! The greater part of Christians are sad and sorrowful; and there are only a small number that partake of this Easter peace; the reason of this we shall find in our history.

The disciples at Jerusalem might have partaken of it from the moment when their risen Lord appeared in the midst of them, and uttered his gentle salutation; but alas! instead of doing so, pale and trembling they crowded together, and cried in the utmost fear and anguish—"A spirit! a spirit!" They could not comprehend how their crucified Master could be restored to life; and why could they not comprehend? Because, partly from their own fault the light was wanting which could alone make clear the eternal counsel of the Almighty; and in spite of all the previous instructions of their Master, the aim of his mission to this earth still remained in their eyes a mystery. They knew not yet for what purpose Christ had offered obedience, nor why he had suffered and been put to death. Had they known how to look into those secrets, the re-appearance of Jesus would not have surprised, far less have terrified them; they would have regarded his resurrection as a thing which must necessarily follow his death; and it would have been to them a fountain of peace and joy; while far from trembling at his entrance they would have saluted him with exclamations of delight. Even in the present day, my brethren, the cause why so few believers partake of that Easter peace which is so freely offered to them, may be traced to their want of gospel-light preventing them taking clear views of the subject. Most true it is that they love the Lord Jesus, and believe in him, but they know not yet all that they possess in him, for it is a knowledge that generally comes but slowly and by degrees. They can give no reason for the hope that is in them; their Christianity wants a sure foundation; they have too little Bible knowledge to support them; Jehovah remains concealed from them in his holy temple; and they are still groping in darkness with regard to the weightiest and most important articles of our faith—the representation of Christ, our justification by him, and union with him. Alas! it is a thing unknown, how God views them as perfect in Christ, pure, spotless, and worthy of his love: and thus it is impossible for their hearts to enjoy Easter peace, since the spring and fountain of it is concealed from them.

After the Saviour has, with infinite pains, brought the disciples to the state when they begin to believe that he has actually returned to life, and that it is he who now stands in the midst of them; the peace which is even now about to enter their hearts turns back, for it finds no resting-place. In a most unexpected manner the spark of faith is all but extinguished; for, as our history informs us, they do not believe from excess of joy. "No," think they, "if the shining form before us be actually Christ, he must have risen from the dead to be restored to us, and we should then be too happy! Such rapture and delight would indeed be overpowering; for it would be a heaven upon earth!" Thoughts such as these prove that they have already some idea of Easter happiness; and because they feel that if Jesus lived it would be bliss unutterable, they come to the conclusion that it cannot be He whom they now behold: it is, indeed, touching and heart-moving to see how they cannot believe for wonder and joy. Answer me, my friends, are not such strange conclusions but too common in the church of Christ? Have you not observed that when we praise and exalt those possessions which have been assured to us in the testament of our great Pledge, and when we speak with joy of those privileges and rights which are ours through Christ, many of the brethren reply, "No, that were too much for poor sinners! Were this really the case, the Christian might go through life rejoicing, having nothing to fear, nothing to care for, and nothing to annoy!" This is their opinion; and instead of searching the word of truth to discover if such be truly the case, they remain inert, believing not for astonishment, and thus rendering it impossible for the Easter peace to enter their hearts. Ye fools, do ye not know that it is the glory of the Son of God to have attained for his people that which is perfect, full, and incomparable? It is your narrow and contracted hearts which have prevented you viewing this in its proper light; and the very fulness and completeness of the gifts which we receive, may well manifest to us that it is not a man, but the King of kings, who has adopted and made us his own.

There is another impediment which prevents Easter peace flowing into our souls; and this is our own self-righteousness. We fancy it to be connected with a certain progress in holiness, as if by fulfilling certain moral obligations we could prove ourselves qualified for its enjoyment before receiving it; and certainly there is a species of preparation required, but it consists in a deep and lively feeling of our own sinfulness and misery, nothing else being necessary. The disciples in our history were misled by similar false ideas, which retarded their progress towards a calm and serene Easter life. They thought, "If Christ were indeed risen from the dead, he would not have come into the midst of us with the salutation of peace upon his lips, after we had so shamefully denied and forsaken him. It might have been otherwise had we remained faithful to him, then . . . . ." Alas! they contemplate Easter peace as a thing to be purchased by their own good works. " What does it cost? O ye fools! The peace of Easter is indeed above all price; Jesus, however, offers it to you as the gift of grace; it is not as saints, but as sinners, that he invites you to partake; and all that desire it have a right to it, and may drink deep draughts of its heavenly wine.

III. Thus you see that the barriers are many and various which close the heart against Easter joy. Let me now try to remove them, and prepare a path for its entrance into your bosoms. Let me in the first place entreat you to consider how anxious our Saviour appears to be that the peace which he has so dearly purchased should not remain unenjoyed, but on the contrary flow like a stream over our souls, and transport us with rapture up to heaven. Scarcely has he shaken off the icy chains of death, than we behold him on the road to dry the tears of the hopeless and afflicted, and to breathe his peace into the hearts of the mourners. This is henceforward his sole occupation, and his only care. " Peace be unto you!" is every where his first salutation; and all his actions have the establishment of this peace for their aim. See how diligently he is employed in our text, striving to convince his alarmed disciples that it is indeed he who now stands in the midst of them; and, by means of this conviction, to lead into their hearts the stream of Easter peace. He first addresses them by the simple question, " Why are ye troubled? And why do thoughts arise in your hearts?" Then he shows them his hands and his side, to convince them that it is he himself who stands in the midst of them. " Handle me and see," he cries, "for a spirit hath not flesh and bones, as ye see me have!" And when they still would not believe, he asked them, "Have ye here any meat?" And they gave him a piece of a broiled fish, and of an honey-comb. And he took it and did eat before them, in order that their doubts might cease, and that they might be enabled to give themselves up entirely to joy. It is the wish of our Saviour also, that we likewise whom he purchased with his blood should enjoy his peace; we must therefore no longer ask, "Dare we feel this peace?" For our Lord himself has said, "Peace I leave with you; my peace I give unto you!" And the words of the Apostle Paul are, "Rejoice in the Lord alway; and again I say, Rejoice!" Observe also, my friends, who the persons are to whom the Saviour offers his Easter peace. Are they the saints? Are they the people who have fought a good fight, who have finished their course, and who have kept the faith? Certainly, if we view them in Christ, they have done so; but in their own persons they are faithless, unbelieving, and their virtues have suffered shipwreck; when their love came to be tried it could not stand the proof, for they had nothing to bring forward but lamentations for their weakness, their sinfulness, and their errors. Did this, however, prevent our Lord offering them the whole fruit of his sufferings and of his death? Did they hear a single word of reproach from his mouth? Did he make any conditions with them, saying, "As soon as ye have performed this or that, the same peace shall enliven you which I now enjoy!" No, it was far otherwise; not a syllable of the kind was heard; not the faintest allusion to the performance of the law; he advanced to meet them with the utmost condescension and love; and greeted them in the simple words, "Peace be unto you!"

IV. We must never forget the manner in which Jesus established and confirmed this peace in the hearts of his disciples. He carried them directly to the Scriptures; for we read in verse 44th, "And he said unto them, These are the words which I spake unto you, whilst I was with you, that all things must be fulfilled which were written in the law of Moses, and in the Prophets, and in the Psalms, concerning me. Then opened he their understanding, that they might understand the Scriptures, and said unto them, Thus it is written, and thus it behoved Christ to suffer, and to rise from the dead the third day: and that repentance and remission of sins should be preached in his name among all nations, beginning at Jerusalem." Yes, my brethren, Jesus carries his disciples to the word. And now I call on you to go and do likewise. What is the origin of the peace which most of our Christians enjoy? Alas! its roots are in the sand; it takes its rise from mere feeling and emotion; and therefore it resembles the grass, which no sooner springs up than it withers and dies. As long as they have some one to enliven their faith, as long as they have devotional excitement, they are happy and at peace; but when they no longer receive those external impulses, or when habit has deadened their effect, then the heaven of their souls is overcast with clouds, and storms begin to arise. Their peace has its foundation in the waters, and there is no firm ground under their feet.

There is a foolish misunderstanding also among our Christians; they confound peace and idleness, regarding the sabbath-like rest which we preach, as a flat contradiction to that holy activity which ought to manifest itself in our lives, and on this account they reject with mistrust our invitation to the enjoyment of the sweetest fruit which grows upon the gospel-tree. Strange delusion! Have they not read in Philippians, "The peace of God, which passeth all understanding, shall keep your hearts and minds through Christ Jesus?" And in Galatians, "But the fruit of the Spirit is love, joy, peace?" Do they not remember also how our Lord himself has in a manner joined together peace and activity? for immediately after saluting the disciples in the words, "Peace be unto you!" he adds, "As my Father hath sent me, even so send I you." Indeed we cannot mistake what our Lord evidently intended to show us, that the latter injunction is the consequence of the reception of his peace. After he had breathed it into the hearts of the disciples, he gave them the commission to impart it to others in all parts of the world. It is like the honey on Jonathan's rod, enlightening the eyes; or like the bread which Elias received in the desert, making the knees strong. What gave Paul his power to overcome the world, and his unwearied zeal for the service and honour of his Master? What inspired Stephen and James with courage to sacrifice their lives in the cause of the gospel? Was it not the peace of Christ which reigned in their hearts? While enjoying it no command was too severe for them to execute; no bulwark too strong for them to assail; no wall too high for them to climb; no sacrifice too great for them to make. Their whole energy and activity dedicated to the service of God was but the streamlet proceeding from the divine fountain of peace in their souls. "We see," says Luther, "that those who have a cheerful and contented spirit, and whose hearts are pervaded by joy and peace, have also strength and activity. Nothing is too heavy for them to bear, and their joy flows like a refreshing stream through their whole body, enlivening and quickening it." Solomon says also, "A merry heart maketh a cheerful countenance; but by sorrow of the heart the spirit is broken."

Remember this, my brethren, and throw down that barrier of prejudice and blindness which has been built so foolishly to oppose the progress of the river of Easter peace. Rejoice because even on this side of Jordan a Horeb stands inviting your ascent, and do not let yourselves doubt that God has appointed you to commence here below that great Sabbath which awaits you above. Banish from your souls all false terror of Sinai; cast from you a diffidence for which there is no cause; and in child-like simplicity pluck the fruit which grew for you, and take with thankfulness that cup of peace presented to you by the Prince of Easter!

THE OFFICE OF THE HOLY SPIRIT

1 Cor. iii. 16

Know ye not that ye are the temple of God, and that the Spirit of God dwelleth in you?

Well may we be astonished at the terms in which the Apostle Paul speaks of the children of the new covenant. Never were such things written of the Old-Testament saints as are now written of the people under the gospel dispensation. What then says the apostle? He maintains that those who are regenerated are the temple of God, and that the Holy Spirit, the renewer of the world, has his dwelling-place within them. On another occasion also he says, "Know ye not that your body is the temple of the Holy Ghost?" Showing plainly that it is not merely the brethren taken collectively who are so, but that each member of the community is a temple. Let us now inquire what the apostle means when he speaks of the Holy Spirit and of his living temple; and let us contemplate the Comforter as resembling Solomon in building—Bezaleel in adorning—and, lastly, Aaron in officiating as high-priest.

I. The Holy Spirit builds; this is his occupation when we first learn to know him, and certainly we often behold him employed in it. He resembles the man in the well-known parable of our Lord, who dug deeply; and like him also he lays the foundation of his house upon a rock. There is a city existing upon earth, which has nowhere its equal: it consists of holy sanctuaries and temples; it is invisible and yet close at hand; and the world contemns it, although it is the most glorious thing in it. The wings of Eternal Love are spread over it; heaven smiles on it benignantly; its walls and ramparts are of fire, and its foundations are firm as the eternal mountains. It is the city of the King of kings, and it is the office of the Holy Spirit to raise and extend it. He is a builder of temples; and in this point of view he stands in the same relation to Christ that Solomon did to David. The latter by his victories and conquests first rendered the building of the temple possible; he also provided the materials, and sketched the plan which Solomon put into execution.

No one is by nature a temple; on the contrary, by nature we are the dwelling-places of an evil spirit, who has his work in the hearts of the unregenerated, and who blinds them so that they believe a lie. It is now the employment of the Holy Spirit to remodel this living charnel-house, and for this purpose he throws down and raises up; he destroys and creates anew. His instrument is the holy Scriptures; he makes the word penetrating and sharper than a two-edged sword; giving it power to make impression, and animating it with the breath of life. You know from experience how it acts; sometimes it strikes like a thunderbolt, and sometimes it flashes past; two houses stand together, the one is struck, while the other is untouched:—Sunday after Sunday passes by, while the heavy laden clouds of our sermons thunder and lighten over the heads of the people; but what good does it do? They pass away without effect until the Spirit direct them. Then indeed there is a change; the rain falls on the heart; the fiery flames descend, and the word strikes like an invisible sword, reforming and creating anew.

It is melancholy to see a man going on unchanged, and in all respects the same as when he came into the world; but it is still more melancholy when this man is at peace with himself, and satisfied with his own condition. The curse rests upon his head, and—he is at peace! He walks along entangled in the meshes and snares of hell, and—still he is at peace! He is the enemy of God, who is never contemned with impunity—and yet peace and tranquillity are his! Is not this terrible? It is a sure sign that the Holy Spirit has not yet begun to labour in his heart. It may happen, however, that he feels differently; his feelings may resemble those of a bird confined in a cage, which, at the approach of summer, beats with impatience against the bars of its little prison, because it feels that here is not its element, and that, if possible, it must away. When ye hear the voice of an invisible One whispering at every moment, "Ye must be changed, completely changed!—when the words

Death, Judgment, and Eternity, sound in your ears like thunder or the clang of a trumpet, and when there is an end of silence and tranquillity in your bosoms; then all this argues the approach of a blessed change, and that the Holy Spirit has begun his work in your hearts. When the sounds which you hear become still more distinct and articulate; when it seems as though some one thus addressed you, "Verily thou art a sinner!"—when a Nathan whom ye cannot see, brands you as guilty; then indeed ye must not doubt that the Spirit is there. When ye strive to drown the voice of awakening conscience in the noise and tumult of the world; but when from every corner ye hear a voice crying, "Adam, where art thou?—when ye can no longer take refuge in the thought, "God is merciful!" for from the clouds is responded, "and just, and holy, and like a consuming fire!"—when you say to yourself, "I will try to amend!" but when the words are thundered forth, "What canst thou do to redeem thy soul?"—then it is clear that the great Builder has commenced his mysterious work. And when the peace ye once possessed has departed, and the whole world cannot restore it to you; when ye have ceased to enjoy the pleasures of life, because you have no reconciled God to console you; when the fountain of tears begins to flow, and the chamber within re-echoes with sighs and ejaculations of "Mercy, mercy!—Help, Lord Jesus!—O Lord Jesus!" then, indeed, the building of the Spirit is making rapid progress. Let him proceed without interruption, for consider that it is a hovel which is being changed into a temple of God;

and well may there be demolition and destruction, casting down and breaking in pieces. It is as though those wheels which were beheld by Ezekiel were passing through the soul, in whom was the spirit of a living creature, and which were full of eyes penetrating the inmost recesses of the heart.

Then the man who had hitherto regarded himself as blameless, confesses, "I am the chief of sinners!" —then those tears flow from the eyes of the vain and worldly Magdalene, which only one hand in earth or heaven can dry;—then the proud Simon, perceiving his own helplessness, breaks forth into the cry, "Lord, save me!"—the publican, beating his heart, says, "God be merciful to me a sinner!"—and the jailor asks, "What must I do to be saved?" Happy art thou if thou resemblest any one of these; it is a sure sign that much has already been done towards preparing thy heart for the dwelling-place of the Holy Spirit; the hateful guests who formerly made it their habitation, are already banished; sin no more rules over thee, for thou art now at variance with it, and the world no longer enchants thee, for it has lost its allurement. Delusion ceases to possess thy soul; the Spirit has swept away a thousand errors and misconceptions, and He who of his own accord, has with almighty power commenced the good work within thee, will most assuredly finish that which he has begun. Above all, he takes care that the alarmed soul should not altogether despair; and he points out to the bruised heart the true fountain of consolation. It is true that he tears away from beneath your feet the delusive ground of your own strength and righteousness, but only to substitute in its place another and a better foundation. He establishes you and your hopes upon a rock; he declares to you Christ and him crucified ; explains the mystery of his sufferings and death in the stead of wretched sinners; teaches you to trust in his merits only, and kindle that love towards him in your breast, which many waters cannot quench, neither can the floods drown it. Ye are no longer what ye were ; but ye are houses in the city of God, sanctuaries and temples, firmly grounded on a fountain which cannot be shaken, and dedicated to Jehovah and his glory. No one henceforth can assail you,—no one say ought against you,—no one put you in shame; for him that doeth so, saith the apostle, "shall God destroy;" for the temple of God is holy, which temple ye are.

II. When the Holy Spirit has like Solomon finished building the temple, he enters into it to continue his labours, in the manner of Bezaleel. Bezaleel was the artificer full of understanding and wisdom, who was appointed by God to erect the holy tabernacle in the desert, and more particularly to ornament the interior of the tent with rich carving and symbolical images, and to superintend the making of the consecrated furniture. Such an artificer is the Holy Spirit, and he never permits the interior of his living temple to remain empty and unadorned ; he works in every manner, and there is nothing more beautiful than the fruit of his labours. Let us now enter the sanctuary of a regenerated soul, and contemplates its glorious contents.

That which first arrests our attention is a rich carved work, the figures of which remind one of those which decorated the holy tabernacle, or the walls of the temple. There are no longer to be seen pictures of the folly and vanity of the world, arrayed in tempting colours, and alluring us to sin; but in their stead there are pictures of the kingdom of light and of everlasting life. But brighter and in fresher colours than all beside, we see on every hand the picture of Him who is the Alpha and Omega, and the great power which governs the world. In what bold characters has it been drawn, and in what colours of flame has it been painted by the invisible Limner! It is a picture which will remain indelible, for it is eternal as the heart in which it is placed. We behold the fairest among the children of men in all stages of his life, and in the most various situations and circumstances. A beautiful child, he rests in the manger, the pious shepherds bending their knees before him: now he appears as king of the elements, walking upon the sea, and stretching out his hand to save his sinking disciple. There he stands like a conqueror at the grave of Lazarus, the dead becoming alive at his command, and issuing forth from the prison-house of death. Again we behold him comforting Magdalene, entering the house of Zaccheus, curing the sick of the palsy, and feeding the thousand in the wilderness. All these scenes, and many others, shine forth in living pictures from the canvass, and are of wonderful efficacy in sanctifying and purifying the heart: the splendour of a supernatural light illuminates them, and the frames in which they are set are of fire. But if there is one among those pictures of Christ which arrests our attention more than the rest, it is the sufferings of the man of sorrows in his crown of thorns; and next to this his triumph and gladness on the third day as the conqueror of hell and of death. But where should I end were I to describe the second series of pictures in the spiritual temple? They are indeed innumerable, and all the chambers are filled with them. They are representations of the city above, enrapturing pictures of our future glory, apocalyptic sketches of the new and perfect kingdom, and portraits drawn by an inspired hand, of holy men long departed to their eternal homes. And those pictures and images, which in the temple of the soul stand in the place of those cherub forms that ornamented the house at Jerusalem, do not lie dead and inactive, preserved in the caskets of memory. No, they are alive in the heart: the Spirit of life painted them there, and they manifest their activity unceasingly, in enlivening, consoling, and exciting us to piety.

If we look still more closely into our spiritual sanctuary and its various chambers, we perceive beside the pictures many important sentences and inscriptions. They are divine promises, selected from the Book of Life, each one more beautiful than another, all sealed and confirmed by the Holy Spirit, and inscribed in the heart in letters of fire. Here one may read,—"I have loved thee with an everlasting love; therefore with loving-kindness have I drawn thee!" Jer. xxxi. 3. "For the mountains shall depart, and the hills be removed; but my kindness shall not depart from thee, neither shall the covenant of my peace be removed, saith the Lord that hath mercy on thee." Isa, liv. 10. "Fear not; for I have redeemed thee, I have called thee by thy name; thou art mine." Isa. xliii. 1. "My sheep hear my voice, and I know them, and they follow me: and I give unto them eternal life; and they shall never perish, neither shall any man pluck them out of my hand." John x. 27, 28. "When thou passest through the waters, I will be with thee; and through the rivers, they shall not overflow thee: when thou walkest through the fire, thou shalt not be burnt; neither shall the flame kindle upon thee." Isa. xliii. 2.

But we are not yet at an end; for there are still many beautiful things to be viewed in our temple. The Bezaleel from on high has erected an altar within it, upon approaching which, no matter at what time, we invariably perceive the fragrance of a sacrifice; perhaps it may only consist of a faint ejaculation of thanks, or an unconscious sigh of complaint and longing, nevertheless the cloud of incense can always be discerned hovering above it, sometimes even ascending in thick columns, and filling the whole tabernacle. Near the altar of prayer we behold the eternal lamp burning, and the eternal Artificer has not forgotten to adorn it also; deeply engraved upon it, in living characters, we read the words—"In Jesus is salvation, and in no other." This light may be darkened, but it can never be extinguished. Think you that it was actually extinguished in the breast of Simon Peter, when he refused to acknowledge Jesus? I reply, No; it was not extinguished even for a moment. However far astray a regenerated person may wander, it is still impossible that this little flame can be altogether quenched; his soul may look desolate; the altar of prayer in his spiritual temple may lie in ruins, and grass may grow upon its steps; the holy pictures may be obliterated, or be, from their faded colours, no longer recognisable; and the poor heart, once so gloriously adorned, may resemble a forsaken dwelling, where the birds of night find a habitation, and which the rain and the storm penetrate; all this may take place, and yet the lamp of the testimony—"Thou art the Christ!" may still flicker among the ruins in the now desolate hall. The divine flame of this conviction still remains, and will most assuredly, sooner or later, lead back the lost sheep, by the aid of its light, into the arms of its Shepherd.

Have we now finished the examination of the temple? Not yet, my brethren; there are still more of the works of the heavenly Bezaleel. Besides the seven golden candlesticks of the wisdom from on high, we behold in the sanctuary of the regenerated soul, the whole contents of the old covenant. Here is the eternal law, no longer engraved upon tables of stone as formerly, but written by the finger of the Spirit on the fleshly tables of the heart. It has now become the instinct of the heart, and its secret inclination; it no longer constrains, for pleasure and duty now coincide. There is to be found the rod of Aaron always green, always producing flowers and fruit; the priesthood of Christ as comprehended by faith; his eternal mediatorship, affording unceasingly to the conscience its fruits of peace, and from day to day quickening the heart with renewed enjoyment. The little pot with the imperishable manna is not even wanting—the joy of knowing that we are the children of God, and partakers of his grace—divine treasures, in comparison of which whole worlds of temporal glory are as nothing. And what shall I say of the immortal garlands with which the Spirit encircles the pillars and festoons the walls of the temple of the soul? No virtue is here wanting; whatever is just and true—whatever is beautiful and glorious—whatever is lovely and of good report, all are twined together. Humility scatters its violet-odour; the passion-flower of patience turns round in faith, following the course of the Sun of Righteousness; and from the lily-cup of a renewed and heavenly spirit there issues forth the sweet fragrance of those acts of benevolence which are never wanting in the lives of the just. Thus we behold garlands of ever-blooming flowers plucked from the garden of God, watered with heavenly dew, and bound together by the ties of perfection and love.

III. When the Comforter has finished his work in the character of Bezaleel, think you that he will take leave of the temple, and depart from it? No, my brethren; our Saviour has promised that the Comforter will remain with you; and Paul also says, "Know ye not that ye are the temple of God, and that the Spirit of God dwelleth in you?" He now makes it his permanent abode; not a place merely to enter and depart from. A soul which the Son of God has purchased and washed with his own most precious blood, will not be accounted by the Holy Spirit as too mean a domicile. But it is only priests who inhabit a temple; and the Holy Spirit may, in this respect, be regarded as an Aaron performing his priestly functions in the souls of the regenerated.

The priests, as you are aware, had to make use of blood in many things; and in this also the Spirit resembles them. He it is who makes the blood of atonement, which we are by nature unable to perceive, so unutterably costly and precious in our eyes: he teaches us its importance, and enables us by means of faith to comprehend its power; he enables us to appropriate it to ourselves, and he sprinkles it on the floors of our hearts, making us hear its voice, which cries louder than that of Abel. And by whom do we enjoy such peace in this blood, that no contemplation of the holiness of God, no thought of the multitude of our sins, is able to lessen it? It is by the Holy Spirit, the Comforter, the High-Priest, and the sprinkler of blood. The offices of this invisible Aaron are of various kinds; and who could name or recount them all! Sometimes he stands with the incense kindled in his hand, his eyes raised to heaven, and in the attitude of prayer; for all the devotion whose incense ascends from our souls, is kindled by his breath of life. He gives it substance, and he gives it wings; he warms and enables it to rise. At other times he rings the bell of the sanctuary; then suddenly, as though some miraculous trumpet had been blown, the congregation of our thoughts assemble clad in their Sunday apparel. He preaches to them, unfolds one mystery after another to their comprehension, explains texts, parables and histories, and pours out light and joy upon all. We behold him again performing his office at the altar: he sacrifices, and it is a thank-offering which he presents: "Give thanks unto the Lord," he cries with a loud voice, "for he is good!" Then it is a sacrifice of praise: "Bless the Lord, O my soul, and forget not all his benefits!" When we bring a burnt-offering also, that is, when we give up our dearest wishes or most valued possessions for the Lord's sake,—when, to please him, we part with some joy, lay aside some prerogative or some advantage, or account all as shame that we may win Christ when we do so,—it is not we who bring these sacrifices to the altar; but it is He, the invisible Aaron, who does so, and who then burns them in the sight of God. Sometimes he opens the horn of consecrated oil in the soul, when its fragrance fills the whole temple, impregnating even the air without, and manifesting its presence, on every occasion, by words of power, by friendly consolation, or by joyful notes of praise. But we have not yet enumerated all his priestly functions. He spreads forth his hands in blessing; he blesses when our spirits bear testimony that we are the children of God; when our hearts rejoice because we are of a chosen and a royal race; when he declares us to be people in whom there is no longer spot or stain; or when, in short, he enables our hearts to enjoy what the Son purchased for us with his blood. He consecrates, also; and, oh! how beautiful, how lovely, is the temple of the soul when he performs this work! No longer is there any thing impure to be discerned;

our wishes and desires mount upon seraph's wings, far above the high places of this earth; with countenances veiled like those of the angels of God, the thoughts stand solemnly assembled around the throne of the Lamb, and the glory of God fills the house of the soul.

As it belonged to the office of the old-testament priest to stand as representative of the people; so we behold the Priest from on high acting in a similar manner in the temple of the regenerated heart. He not only represents us when he gives form and substance to those sighs which we ejaculate when we know not how or what we would pray for, and when he makes them conformable to the dignity and beauty of the house of God; but in various other ways he is Paraclete and Advocate, Intercessor and Representative. When our conscience is accusing us, and a voice cries out to it, "Why dost thou accuse? God is greater than thou!" who is it that steps forward on our side? Who is it but the Comforter? When some error or iniquity rises in judgment against us, and One who is not of our heart, although he dwell within it, says to the Judge, "Condemn the sin, but not the sinner, for he is holy!" who is it that thus pleads our cause? It is the great advocate within. When we are in perplexity, and know not what we shall say, or how we shall defend ourselves, and when, all of a sudden, we are no longer at a loss for words, but, to our own astonishment, express ourselves at the right moment, and in the most eloquent and appropriate manner, is it not clearly discernible that an invisible being assists us, and furnishes us with words to speak? Thus we see how the Spirit is accustomed to perform his office of Priest in the temple of the soul; his occupations are innumerable, and he labours without ceasing.

Meanwhile it may happen to us with the Aaron in our souls, as it did to the Jewish congregation with their priest Zacharias; he may disappear, when one least expects it, from the front of the soul's temple; he may vanish in the back-ground of the sanctuary, and the congregation of the thoughts may stand anxious and trembling before the curtain, afraid lest he have died, or, at least, that he may no more return. Oh! then, be still, ye despairing thoughts; if ye would only listen attentively, ye would hear, though at a distance, the music of the bell at the hem of his garment! In some way or other, perhaps in a sigh from the depths of the heart, or in a longing desire for the Lord, its sound will be borne to your ears, and be to you a joyful and satisfactory token that the priest still remains in the temple; and before ye are awake, he steps once more out of his concealment, the censer of incense or the harp in his hand, and convinces you anew of the truth of our Saviour's promise which he gave to his disciples, that the Comforter should abide with them always.

Thus the Spirit performs his various offices; he builds in the desert places,—renovates that which is decayed and withered,—fills our hearts with his decorations, and joins with them even in the great and eternal song, "Worthy is the Lamb that was slain to receive power, and riches, and wisdom, and strength, and honour, and glory, and blessing! Amen."

THE CHRISTIANS AFTER THE FEAST OF PENTECOST

ACTS II. 41—47

Then they that gladly received his word were baptized; and the same day there were added unto them about three thousand souls. And they continued steadfastly in the apostles' doctrine and fellowship, and in breaking of bread and in prayers. And fear came upon every soul; and many wonders and signs were done by the apostles. And all that believed were together, and had all things common; and sold their possessions and goods, and parted them to all men, as every man had need. And they, continuing daily with one accord in the temple, and breaking bread from house to house, did eat their meat with gladness and singleness of heart, praising God, and having favour with all the people. And the Lord added to the church daily such as should be saved.

WHEN our Saviour said in the Gospel of Matthew, "Among them that are born of women there hath not risen a greater than John the Baptist; notwithstanding, he that is least in the kingdom of heaven is greater than he,"—he meant that there was no one then living, no, not even Peter, James or John, to be compared to his forerunner. In the days when Jesus spake these words, his disciples were in gospel light and illumination, far behind the man who was able even then to cry out, "Behold the Lamb of God, which taketh away the sin of the world!" and who had already found in Christ the friend and bridegroom of his soul. During this period, John the Baptist was most assuredly the greatest of the followers of Christ; but there came a time when even the least among the Christians was greater than John; and it commenced on the great day whose remembrance we solemnize by the festival of Whit-Sunday—I mean the day of Pentecost. Now, for the first time, that which our Lord expressed by the words, "the kingdom of heaven," was actually to be seen upon earth: the new-testament church came into existence; and it was those who were, spiritually speaking, born on the Feast of Pentecost, to whom our Lord referred in the expression, "he that is least in the kingdom of heaven." How deep, and at the same time how true, do his words now appear! for, in all respects, the humblest brother in this newly-founded church stood higher than John. But methinks I hear you inquire, Was the church of the faithful different then from what it was previously? It was so in more than one respect. The Holy Spirit, as well as Christ himself, now stood in quite a new and different relation to believers; and it naturally followed that the life of those men, spiritually as well as externally, should also assume a new and different form. That *new thing* which, according to the ancient prophets, the Lord was to do upon earth, was now accomplished; for a church similar to that which had just sprung into existence, had never before been seen upon earth. Of this we shall easily convince ourselves, by contemplating, for a few moments, the first Christian community at Jerusalem. The first thing which arrests our attention, is the efficacy of the Holy Spirit exemplified in a new manner, showing the commencement of a new period in God's government. *The form and manner of the church's establishment is new: the spiritual and external life of its members has a new aspect; and their spiritual influence upon others is also new.*

I. Has any thing more beautiful taken place since the beginning of the world, than the glorious planting of the word which we contemplate to-day? The life of heaven seems indeed to have established its dwelling-place in this vale of tears. A community, dedicated to God, consisting of three thousand souls; but a community such as neither Moses, Elias, nor any of the ancient saints had ever beheld. Alas! the country where this living memorial of the grace of God and of the creative power of his Holy Spirit once stood, is now waste and desert, surrounded by the confusion of Babel and the barbarism of the crescent; and what is still more melancholy, this flower-garden of earth has entirely disappeared, and nowhere is to be found any thing approaching to the beauty and glory in which it flourished at first in Jerusalem. The church of our times, in comparison to the apostolic, resembles a field whose verdure has been dried up and withered; the model of this temple of God, however, still remains preserved to us. It has not only been saved from oblivion in the writings of the apostles, but the hand of God is always depicting it in fresh colours. Not only does the Almighty continue to build according to this beautiful model; but, in the same fashion, that glorious building will be erected whose image is already faintly discernible in the mirror of prophecy, whose golden pillars shall extend from pole to pole, and whose circumference shall span the whole earth, from the rising up of the sun to its going down. It must, therefore, be of the greatest importance for us to contemplate the original form of the church of Christ, and to examine minutely the peculiar character of the first Christian community.

Even the manner in which this church was founded may well surprise us. Whether we contemplate the instruments who effected it, the means which the pouring out of the Holy Spirit called into existence, the rapidity with which the building proceeded, or the foundation on which this beautiful temple was erected, we must indeed confess that nothing similar had ever taken place before, and that a new era had most certainly begun. The instrument who effected this was, as you are aware, a poor fisherman from the Galilean sea,—a man whose mind had been formed in no prophetic school, much less exercised in the task of converting and instructing; and who had been, only a few short days before, so poor in spirit, so ignorant, and so unqualified for speaking, that at first sight Simon seemed the most unfit to be entrusted with the establishment of a new church, particularly one which was to be formed from such stubborn materials as an antichristian community. And yet it is this same Simon, whose tongue, like an all-powerful sceptre, lays three thousand souls prostrate in the dust at the feet of Jesus, and commences a complete revolution in the spiritual world, such as there is nothing to be compared to in previous history, not even in that of the most glorious instruments whom God employed in olden time, with all their dazzling eloquence, and the miracles which stood at their command. This circumstance shows us that we have arrived at a new period in God's government. We behold here the actual presence in this world of the Holy Spirit, and a new form of his efficacy and miraculous agency, such as we do not find mentioned in sacred history as having taken place in any previous age of the world.

The means by which the first Christian church was called into existence was the word. But what sort of word?—a word like that of Noah, when he threatened the children of men that a deluge of water should overwhelm them, and that the Spirit of God would no longer strive with them? Or a word like that of Moses, "Cursed be he that continueth not in all the words of this law, to do them!" Or like the prediction of Jonah, "Yet forty days, and Nineveh shall be overthrown!" No, it was none of these; it was neither a curse-bringing, a thundering, nor a destroying word, although it was unutterably powerful and penetrating. It was a word which healed at the same moment that it wounded; and raised up and exalted the instant it cast down: it excited neither fear nor anguish, but, on the contrary, melted the heart and kindled love: it was the word of the cross—the message of salvation in Christ.

Ye remember the sermon of Peter, that Jesus who was crucified has been made by God both Lord and

Christ, and that whosoever will call on his name shall be saved, and receive the gift of the Holy Spirit! This was the sum of his discourse, and this constituted its weight and impression, its power and sharpness. During the Old Testament time, the sleepers were awakened by the thunders of the law; the gospel of the future Saviour was then only preached to the afflicted as a consolation, and not employed to awaken and arouse the dead, for as yet it was too dark, and veiled in too much obscurity. It was its accomplishment which first gave it the power of penetrating and softening the heart. Nevertheless, during the days of the old covenant, the time had been clearly predicted when friendly lips should preach glad tidings to the nations, when a glorious gospel should call dry bones into life, and when a people should be born unto the Lord, not under the terrors of Sinai, unto bondage, but amidst the gentle breezes of Horeb, to the freedom of children and heirs with Christ. This time commenced with the day of Pentecost; and it is a strange battle-array in which the ministers of God henceforth enter the field against you. We come no more with excommunications; no longer saying to the host of the Lord, "Cursed be he who does this or that!" Instead of approaching you with the pictures of a fearful judgment, and the raging flames of hell, we now advance to meet you with a cup filled with tears and drops of blood,—with a crown of thorns,—with a heart of love pierced by the sword of sin,—and with a bloody cross. "See!" we cry, "this crown was worn by the Son of the living God, in order that you might receive a heavenly diadem!

these tears were shed by Eternal love, that you might be happy and rejoice for evermore!" It is thus we come, the heralds of the new covenant; but, at the same time, no one is safe before us; our arms of might will break the stony heart of the most hardened wretch who fears neither God nor man; the most obdurate soul, whom no admonition and no threatening could move, when attacked by our weapons, falls, a sobbing and penitent child, into the arms of Jesus. Inspired with life by the breath of the gospel, those forms hitherto dead arose, who formed the first community at Jerusalem; it was a new species of resurrection, but henceforward a customary one; the word of the cross was now to evangelize the world, and call the spiritually-dead out of their graves. Wherever the word is preached in all its simplicity and clearness, that Christ is our representative, that "Christ hath redeemed us from the curse of the law, being made a curse for us!"—the justification of sinners by faith and not by works, and the accomplishment of the same through the sacrifice of Jesus once offered;—when this is proclaimed, and when this is heard, there arise alterations and reforms in the characters of men; for it is by means of these words that the Spirit operates, and it is through their preaching that he performs his miracles of spiritual creation.

Although there may be no terror, and the hair may not stand on end at the sound of these words, yet there is an inexpressible melting and softening of the heart;—although there may be no fear and anguish, as amidst the thunders of the law, yet there is a prostration in the dust at the feet of Jesus;—although the limbs may not tremble, yet silent tears are dropping, which Jesus numbers;—and although we do not cry out as on Mount Sinai, "I exceedingly fear and quake!" we say what is far better, "Lord Jesus, I am thine for ever! If I only possess thee, I ask nothing more either in earth or heaven!"

The establishment of the first christian church appears surprising also when we contemplate its unexampled rapidity. Peter had not preached many moments when the greatest change took place; the desert bloomed, and three thousand dead became alive: never before had such things happened. How long were the prophets of old obliged to labour; how long must they exhort and entreat, cry and thunder, before they succeeded in leading one lost sheep out of error, or in bending one knee in true devotion before the throne of Jehovah! And even when they had so far succeeded, it often happened that ere they had time to depart, their toils broke asunder and their prey escaped them. In Jerusalem, on the contrary, all this wonderful draught of fishes remained secure; and what is still more extraordinary, the souls so lately won burst forth at once into a perfect life in the Lord, and henceforward stood with the apostles, as they themselves bear testimony, on an equal height of spiritual illumination and grace. It is impossible to deny that an entirely new operation of the Spirit here took place: he had never laboured in times past so joyfully and so powerfully; and never had he thus manifested himself to sinners, penetrating the heart and creating anew. How can we explain this? Had the house of God not been hitherto prepared for it? Or had the wings of the Spirit been first loosed and set free by the perfecting of the works of reconciliation? Or had his love towards sinners only been fully kindled, on beholding them clad before God in the beauty of their perfect Representative? Or did he now perform to the world his office of manifesting the Son of Man, and his work of atonement, more powerfully, more comprehensively, and more clearly, as a testimony how completely the great Pledge had succeeded in opening for sinners the path to the wished-for goal? Let the cause be what it may, it is enough that with the feast of Pentecost commenced a new period in the history of the agency of the Holy Spirit; and that henceforward more speedy conversions and more perfect results took place.

What, then, was the foundation on which the first christian church at Jerusalem was built? On that of the apostles' teaching. Even this was new! All obscurity was now taken away; the temple of God was no longer raised upon the dark and ambiguous sentences of the prophets, but on the crystalline foundation of simple and unveiled truth. Instead of that symbolical wisdom with which the ancients had been obliged to content themselves, the church now possessed the treasures of divine revelation, both by means of oral communication and by writing: the trumpet whose notes had hitherto instructed them, gave forth a clearer and more intelligible sound; and that which their forefathers had beheld faintly sketched and afar off, now assumed to the eyes of their spirit a clear and distinct appearance. They stepped forth out of the twilight of prophecy into the bright noon-day light of its accomplishment; and might with reason repeat the words of the disciple, "Now speakest thou plainly, and speakest no proverb!" The truths of the gospel were now lowered to the level of human comprehension, while during the days of the old covenant they had been raised to such a height amid the clouds of prophetic inspiration, that the eye could scarcely discern them. People could now, on the contrary, press around them and contemplate them nearly; for they knew what they possessed and believed; and the precious stones of doctrine were now divested of their coverings, and lay clearly displayed to the gaze of all beholders. The brightness and joy of perfect day took the place of the hopes and anticipations of the previous twilight; and instead of sighs and longings, and impatient expectation, the church enjoyed the delight and pleasure of possession.

II. We have already contemplated the strange and wonderful establishment of the first christian community; let us now consider their spiritual and social life. We perceive a sweet-smelling savour wafted around us, like the fragrance of a field which the Lord has blessed; and everywhere we turn our eyes, something totally new and unexampled arrests our attention. In the first place, the whole form of their spiritual life appears new; and yet there never was any want of spiritual life in Israel: what holy and pious men were Moses, Samuel, David, Elijah, and many other servants of God in the ancient world! What heroes of the faith! Brows encircled with the radiancy of another world! Beacons shining through the night of time, and casting forward their radiancy to coming centuries! But of what avail is all this? They were saints of a different kind; and this the Saviour himself testified, when, his disciples wishing to call down fire from heaven as Elias did, he said unto them, "Ye know not what manner of spirit ye are of!" You will easily perceive in what the difference consisted when I put their characters to the proof. If, in enumerating the virtues of the ancient saints, I praise the firmness with which they resisted the allurements of the world; the stedfast faith in which they relied upon God; the earnestness with which they strove to fulfil the demands of the law; and their fiery zeal for the honour of Jehovah,—you must allow that these men of God did indeed possess those virtues; but if I continue my praises in the following words, "How glorious those ancient saints appeared as the living images of the Son of Man! Jesus was reflected in their characters, their whole lives bore the seal and impress of the Lamb, and his spirit was manifested in all their words and actions!"—then you interrupt me; "No!" I hear you cry, "the colours of thy picture are false, and this is not the description of the saints of the Old Testament!" Most assuredly you are right.—The community in whose character the image of the Lamb was reflected, and out of whose form and constitution the splendour of the fairest of the children of men beamed forth—who, imitating the humility of their Lord, made themselves as servants—who received the poor and wretched with the arms of the tenderest compassion—who, when stoned by their enemies, instead of cursing them, said, "Lord, lay not this sin to their charge!"—who repaid the wrath of their persecutors with prayers and intercessions for them—who, with the simplicity of children, were contented to be led by their Lord whithersoever he would, and to be moulded according to his pleasure like clay in the hands of the potter; men such as these were not to be met with during the days when Sinai was clad in its terrors; and they did not appear until a later and a milder time, when the miracle at the feast of Pentecost summoned them into life. It is true, the virtues of those who were then born again were called by the same names as the virtues of the ancient saints; nevertheless they were of a totally different species, and have a different colouring, form, and character, being far more beautiful and more heavenly. Nevertheless I say nothing in disparagement of the ancient saints: far from it! I only maintain that nothing resembling the community of Jerusalem blooms for us amidst the shadows of the law. One can discern in the children of the day of Pentecost the image of the Lamb who purchased and redeemed them; while in the character of the ancient saints, the fiery beams of that Majesty shine forth, in whose presence they stood with their countenances veiled. If you compare together Deborah and Magdalene, Elijah and John, you will easily perceive what I mean.

The love and brotherly unity which subsisted between the members of the community at Jerusalem strikes us also as something entirely new. They are of one heart and one mind ; and a bond of affection unites those flowers of heaven together, such as the ancient saints never felt or witnessed. When we think, however, of Jonathan and David, of Elijah and Elisha, who can doubt that they loved each other in God ? But they did not depend on each other, or live in each other's affection, like the brethren and sisters after the feast of Pentecost. It was altogether impossible for them, and they could not have done it, for many reasons. In the first place, it had not been manifested to the ancient saints, as it afterwards was to those in Jerusalem, how unutterably the Lord loved them, and the secret had not been disclosed which makes that love so powerful ; for it was only after the feast of Pentecost that the Holy Spirit manifested in what a mysterious manner Christians are united together so as to form one body with Christ : He the head and they the members ; no one greater and no one inferior to the rest ; and each equally near and equally dear to the Lord Jesus. No one now possessed any thing, whether temporal or spiritual, for himself alone, but looked upon it as common property. When any happy circumstance occurred to one of the brethren, the others rejoiced as though it had happened to all ; for they regarded it as their Saviour's salutation of love to the whole body. In like manner, when aught unfortunate befel one of their number, they all suffered. The thought was ever present in their souls, "One God shed his blood for all !" They constantly felt, "One arm of love encircles us!" And they had the perpetual consciousness, "On one bosom we recline, in one heavenly book our names stand written, and our cottages of peace are erected together in the same glorious forest of palms!" Those thoughts and feelings which the saints of old never could have enjoyed, were like oil to the love of the brethren; and how must they have strengthened their bond of love! They no longer knew each other after the flesh; but valuing their brethren according to what they were in Christ, beheld them clad in the garments of his righteousness, and altogether beautiful and glorious. How easy was it for them in this point of view to overlook personal errors and failings; and what a powerful means of preventing any bitterness or ill-will, when they were compelled to rebuke and reprimand one another! Each possessed righteousness in his representative, though not in himself; and for this reason willingly gave up his old Adam to be judged, seeing that his own and glorious property could not be taken away from him. He had no need to prize his own rags, since he knew himself to be clad in the raiment of the King of kings. Thus all these things were a powerful assistance to the brotherly love of the saints at Jerusalem, raising around it a barrier and a rampart which nothing could shake, and nothing destroy. Happy community! Glorious bond of union! Oh, that this love, which subsisted in the early ages, might return again, and that peace and concord might be restored to the church of Christ!

If you look upon the social life of the Christians

after the feast of Pentecost, you must confess that here also is something new and altogether unprecedented in the land. The believers are described as breaking bread from house to house, eating their meat with gladness and singleness of heart; praising God, and having favour with all the people. From this picture there shines forth a New Testament light, in more than one respect. A necessity for brotherly intercourse, a consecration of daily life, a social cheerfulness, and a holy gladness and freedom, such as the ancient patriarchs never knew. The brethren at Jerusalem often met together; and why did they do so? Because they had far more numerous and more glorious things to relate than the lonely pilgrims during the days of the law. Each time they ate together in their cottages was like a solemn feast-day; for they knew that their Saviour was in the midst of them, as he had promised; and hence each house was a temple, the chamber where they met a sanctuary, the table an altar, and each morsel of bread a pledge of the love of Him who, though invisible, sat amongst them.

It would have seemed like blasphemy to the ancient saints had they prayed, "Come, Jehovah, and let thy presence be amongst us!" They only knew the Almighty in the clouds, on the wings of the storm, in the smoke of the sanctuary, behind the curtain, or over the cherubim; but of Jehovah under the humble roofs of their cottages, in their chambers, and at their social table, they knew nothing. The time had not yet arrived which was alluded to in the well-known words of Zechariah, "In that day shall there be upon the bells of the horses, Holiness unto the Lord; and the pots in the Lord's house shall be like the bowls before the altar. Yea, every pot in Jerusalem, and in Judah, shall be holiness unto the Lord of hosts; and all they that sacrifice shall come and take of them, and seethe therein." It was on the wings of the Pentecost miracle that those happy days first descended to the reconciled earth. Eating their meat in gladness and singleness of heart, was the characteristic trait of the New-Testament saints: no longer was said, "Touch not this, and touch not that!" and the vexatious ceremonies of the law, having fulfilled their object, were no more required. Henceforth that which entered the mouth was not unclean, since by means of bread and wine they received spiritual grace, the grace of Him who gave them their heavenly food. Far from regarding monastic gloom as the sacrifice which a God of happiness required, they gave themselves up with a free conscience to gladness and cheerfulness. They did as the Apostle James recommends: "Is any merry? let him sing psalms." And they rejoiced in the Lord always, remembering that sadness and gloom are unsuitable to the new covenant.

When we read in our text, "All that believed were together, and had all things common; and sold their possessions and goods, and parted them to all men, as every man had need;" we not only behold the mutual love which prompted them to regard the whole community as one person; but we perceive a superiority to earth, and a freedom from earthly cares, of which there is no trace in the biographies of the Old Testament. There is another novelty which strikes us, for the first time, after the day of Pentecost: the ancient saints seem to have regarded a long life upon earth as the most desirable of blessings; and the cry, "Take me not away in the midst of my days!" rose from their lips with the most impressive earnestness towards heaven. This is not to be wondered at. The hope of living to behold the fulfilment of one or other of those blessed promises which greeted them from afar, rendered dear to them their residence in this vale of tears; while, on the other hand, the view beyond the grave was so dark and cloudy in those days of the law, that they never had a desire to depart like the New-Testament Christians.

How different were the feelings of the Pentecost assemblage! The ties which bound Israel so fast to this side of the tomb had here been loosened; and the holy curiosity of the ancient patriarchs no longer found a place in the hearts of those children of the new covenant, for they had already beheld the greatest and most glorious thing which ever happened to the world—the incarnation of the Son of God. What the saints of old had regarded as the melancholy descent into the tomb, they looked upon as the most blessed and joyful moment in their whole existence. Death was deprived of its terrors, and their eternal home manifested so clearly, and brought so near by the eye of faith, that it seemed as though they walked much more in heaven above than on earth beneath; or as though they were strangers and pilgrims on a short and rapid journey to another existence. This longing for home filled their hearts unceasingly; and they resembled ships lying in the roads, ready to sail, that are waiting impatiently until a favourable wind shall arise. They desired to depart and be with Christ; and in looking forward to death and the grave, their only emotion was the longing desire that the Angel of Peace might speedily appear. They resembled the boy, of whom many of you have already heard, who, not very long ago, entering the chamber where the corpse of his beloved mother lay, and seeing his play-things, which had been left there by accident, exclaimed, weeping bitterly, "Who will have them?—I want them no longer, for I am going to my mother in heaven!" Even so sounded the voices of those Christians. "Who will have them?" was constantly uttered by their hearts; and they were glad to find in the family ties, which joined the congregation together, an opportunity of disburdening themselves of the cares of their earthly possessions. The highest price did not appear to them too dear, if they could thereby purchase undisturbed peace in the contemplation of their eternal inheritance. Most truly were they a Jerusalem resembling that above! Wherever they went, they who beheld them discerned the morning splendour of eternity shining from their features; and the inscription on their banners always was, "I am a pilgrim here, and a citizen of heaven!"

When we contemplate the new period in God's government which commenced on the day of Pentecost, that which strikes us as the most important and glorious circumstance, is the relation in which the faithful now stood to their covenanted God. No one had hitherto experienced this heartfelt connexion with Jehovah ; and it is perhaps the most peculiar characteristic of the church of the New Testament. "Praising God," are the words in our text, and these words refer to this connexion. But did not the saints of old praise God? Most assuredly they did; yet it is only with regard to the members of the Pentecost congregation that this record of their praising God is preserved: for joy in Jehovah was the foundation of their spiritual life. As for the saints of the old covenant, their sins must also have been forgiven them, or they could not have cried, "Praise the Lord, O my soul!" but whenever they fell into a new error, or committed a new crime, it seemed to them as though the heavens were once more overcast with black thunder-clouds; their souls felt anew the whole weight of God's wrath and terrible indignation; the threatenings of the law deprived them of peace; they no longer ventured to raise their eyes to Jehovah, and were oppressed with sorrow and trembling until they had offered sacrifice, and thereby received consolation. Thus, in constant succession, their minds alternated between the utmost anguish of soul and unutterable peace and tranquillity; and if at times one among them experienced a little longer than usual the consciousness that his punishment had been remitted, and the curse taken away, this was the highest and greatest blessing which he ever enjoyed—his sole consolation and fountain of peace. He beheld in his own person a delinquent deserving death, to whom the King of kings had in mercy granted his life; but that he should be much more than this—that he should stand justified, perfect, and spotless before the Eternal, was a thing unknown to him. The righteousness which we possess in Christ had not yet been manifested, but was veiled in those promises which even then greeted the saints from a distance.

How different were the circumstances of the New Testament Christians! Great and glorious disclosures were made to them by the Spirit; and, illuminated by the full noon-day light of the gospel, they knew precisely the relations in which they were placed.

III. A new creation of God, such as took place in Jerusalem, could not long remain concealed; for it was like a city upon a mountain, or a light upon a high place. In what relation then did they stand to the world, and the world to them? This question leads us to the contemplation of another glory of the Pentecost congregation, which was also new and peculiar. It is said in our text, "having favour with all the people." The people could not refuse them its wonder, veneration, and love: but is it at all important whether the blind world praise or condemn us? As far as we ourselves are concerned it is of little importance, but for the Lord's sake we should desire his name to be great and glorious. Would you not wish that the world might be constrained, even against its will, to confess you were very different from it—that you pursued the right path to the end, and employed your lives for the purpose to which they were given?

Would you not rejoice if the unconverted, and the

enemies of the gospel, were obliged to confess, "Never were there such righteous people as these?" I repeat, that, as far as you yourselves are concerned, it can be of no importance whether or not the world praise your humility, purity, patience, and love; neither case can be to your detriment or advantage. You must remember, however, that you do not live for yourselves, but for Him who purchased you with his blood. You were placed in this world to glorify him; you must praise him by word and deed, and in every thing seek his glory. How well did the community at Jerusalem fulfill their holy calling!—in them the rays of Christ's beauty were reflected, like the image of the sun in the little dew-drop; and they stood a memorial of the grace of God, and of the creative power of his Holy Spirit, such as the world had never previously seen. Every ear that heard, and every eye that beheld, praised them as glorious; they were like a green field which the Lord hath blessed, or like a well-watered garden, in which was every flower of holiness and righteousness. They who approached them perceived the odours and the fragrance of another world; a love, such as grew on no natural soil, greeted them at the threshold; the breezes of Horeb were wafted around them; and instead of the Sinai terrors of the olden time, they were made partakers of that peaceful serenity which flowed like a river of Paradise through the midst of the little flock. Whosoever sought help, received it at the doors of this congregation of God; whosoever required counsel, or needed consolation and rest, found many here to receive him with arms of compassion, and tend him carefully day and night. He who desired to behold a city in this evil world, where, instead of selfishness and deceit, truth and brotherly love had their habitation, only required to visit Jerusalem; and, with whatever prejudices he came, the moment he entered the little community, they were dissipated like the clouds of mist by the morning sun. Thus this new Israel shone as a light in the presence of the Lord, fair as the moon, and beautiful as the morning dawn. Was it wonderful that these children of God found favour with the people? For wherever the divine beauty is reflected, the hearts of all must be won by it.

The life of such a community, endued so richly with the gift of the Holy Spirit, must of necessity manifest itself in apostolic activity. No day, therefore, passed in which its circumference was not extended, and some new name added to the brethren. This was the Jerusalem of which it was written, "Sing, O barren, thou that didst not bear; break forth into singing, and cry aloud, thou that didst not travail with child; for more are the children of the desolate than the children of the married wife, saith the Lord!" And what were the means by which they conquered every heart? It was not by negotiations and treaties, not by eloquent speaking, that they accomplished such great things: their only instrument was the gospel; their own lives were the means of converting many; and the net, with which they caught men, was the influence shed by their holy and devout conduct. Whosoever approached them was constrained to exclaim, "This is none other but the house of God; and this is the gate of heaven!" He was forced to confess that the foundation on which this living temple was built, must be a foundation of truth, and approved of by God; and with irresistible power the conviction was forced upon him, that these people were certainly in possession of the one thing needful. If, after all this, instead of swearing allegiance to their standard, he returned to the world, and to the darkness of the night of sin, he must purchase a hollow tranquillity by the most egregious self-deception, and an arduous struggle against his conscience and his better feelings; while, notwithstanding all his endeavours, a sting would still remain behind. Besides the silent influence which the holy lives of the Pentecost community exercised upon the multitude, they had another mighty engine of conversion, in the signs and miracles which God enabled them to perform, as well as in the soul-arresting announcement of the quickening influences of the word of God in each individual bosom. The preaching of the gospel was accompanied by such an Easter-incense of prayer and intercession, which in the name of Jesus ascended up to heaven, that it was impossible for a blessing not to accompany it. Was it strange, then, that the Lord added to the church daily such as should be saved? This congregation might well have converted the world; for if ever there was an army of redeemed sinners that might make hell tremble, it was here: such a phalanx never having entered the field against it. The whole kingdom of darkness was threatened by this bride of the Lamb; and ere he anticipated it, the prince of the abyss was in danger of beholding the banner of Zion planted on his mightiest stronghold.

We now bid adieu to the Pentecost congregation; but can we help desiring, from the bottom of our hearts, that this temple of God might speedily arise out of its ruins!—that it might please the Lord to renew the image of his first glorious plantation in the christian church! It might soon take place; only grasp the cencer of Christ, ye children of grace; pray fervently in his name; storm the gates of heaven with his own promises; "and give him no rest till he establish, and till he make Jerusalem a praise in the earth." If ye do so, but a short time would elapse until every thing should be changed; the clouds would disperse, the desert would bloom, the wastes would look joyful, and from our mountains would resound the cry of joy and astonishment, "Behold the tabernacle of God among the children of men!" Amen.